Look for other *Show Strides* books:

#1 School Horses and Show Ponies

#2 Confidence Comeback

The Plaid Horse
Canton, New York

Copyright © 2019 by Piper Klemm
The Plaid Horse, Canton, New York

Library of Congress Control Number: 2019902660
Show Strides: Moving Up and Moving On / Piper Klemm
Text by Rennie Dyball
Illustrated by Madeleine Swann Murray

This is a work of fiction. Names, characters, businesses, places, events, locales, and incidents are either the products of the author's imagination or used in a fictitious manner. Any resemblance to actual persons, living or dead, or actual events is purely coincidental.

ISBN: 978-1-7329632-2-1

Illustrations © 2019 by Madeleine Swann Murray
Cover Art by Lynn Del Vecchio

1

It was only seven o'clock on an early June morning, but the air already felt thick as Tally walked out to the pony field. She would be a grumpy mess if she had to be up this early on a weekend for any other reason. But when she was riding, or even just being around horses, it suddenly didn't matter so much.

The horses and ponies at Quince Oaks (Oaks, as the riders called it) didn't come in for breakfast until eight thirty in the summertime, so they were all still grazing way out in the fields. But Tally had come prepared. She opened the gate, shook a handful of grain in a bucket, and waited. The ponies had been gathered out of sight in their paddock, but within seconds, the tops of their heads appeared over the crest of the hill. Hooves thundered as the ponies raced each other to the gate, delighted at the early breakfast.

Tally giggled as she watched Goose, the little gray pony she'd been catch-riding, lead the pack with his ears locked straight ahead and his nostrils flaring. None of the ponies slowed down until they'd made their way over the hilltop. Goose skidded to a stop right in front of Tally.

"Hi, sweet boy! You up for an early ride today?"

Goose dropped his sleek, elegant head into her waiting halter while the other ponies nosed around for the grain. Tally chucked the contents of the bucket off to the side so the ponies wouldn't crowd her. As the ponies sniffed around in the grass for the pellets, Tally swiftly opened the gate, allowed Goose to slip out, and reclipped the chain around the fence post. The grain had already been gobbled up and half a dozen pony faces gazed at her expectantly.

"Sorry, guys! You'll come in for breakfast soon." One of the ponies whinnied defiantly as Tally walked away from the field, but Goose didn't seem to notice. Tally often wondered if Goose preferred the company of people to ponies.

She'd only been riding him since the winter, but Tally had already formed a close bond with Goose, a green sales pony currently owned by her trainer, Ryan McNeil. Tally was tasked with taking lessons on Goose (G for short) and showing him in the

children's pony division. It had been less than a year since she started riding with Ryan and catch-riding ponies for him. Before that, she had taken lessons at the Oaks riding school, and had gotten her start competing in the at-home schooling shows.

"I missed you, buddy," Tally said, petting G's neck as they walked out of the sun and into the dim barn. She'd only been out of town for a couple of days, but it felt far longer.

Tally let Goose into his stall to pee—and do whatever else ponies did after coming in from turnout—and she took her time gathering up his grooming supplies and tack. She smiled at the new addition on the Field Ridge photo collage on the wall—a candid picture of her friend Mackenzie Bennett, Mac for short, and her flashy chestnut pony with their ribbon at Devon last week. In the photo,

Joey (show name: Smoke Hill Jet Set), eyes the ribbon on his bridle while Ryan, the girls' trainer, gives Mac a hug. It was such a fun day for Tally and Mac, who had become fast friends when Mac and Joey moved to Quince Oaks.

New to showing on the A Circuit, Tally saw the Devon Horse and Pony Show as the stuff of fantasy, something that she may never have the chance to experience herself. But watching her friend compete there, and ride so well after getting off to a tough start, was a huge motivator.

In a few hours, Tally was scheduled for a working student shift on the school side of the barn. But she'd asked Ryan about riding beforehand, and he gave her the go-ahead to hack Goose as well as two other ponies whose owners wouldn't be riding that weekend.

"Will you hate me if we do some work before your breakfast today, buddy?" Tally asked G, who popped his head up in the stall to address her. Instead of putting him on the cross ties like usual, she let him keep munching on his hay. Since she'd be delaying his breakfast, it seemed only fair to groom him in his stall. Tally wanted to get the pony to the ring before his friends started coming in from the field, which would surely be a big distraction for him.

In the large indoor ring, on a hill above the Oaks barn, Tally walked a lap on a loose rein before picking up some contact and putting the pony to work. They trotted and cantered some circles and around the length of the ring. When Goose noticed the horses starting to come in for breakfast, Tally focused on shortening and lengthening his stride to keep his attention. After only twenty minutes of work,

Goose's shoulders glistened with sweat. Tally gave him a big pat and finished the ride the way they'd started, with a long, loose walk.

"You ready to show again, G? I am," Tally said as the pony's ears flicked back at her. She rubbed the length of his neck and he shook his head from side to side, his silvery mane flipping back and forth. Near the gate, Tally dismounted and ran her hand down the front of G's chest. He was slightly damp, but cool to the touch. And he was very ready for his breakfast.

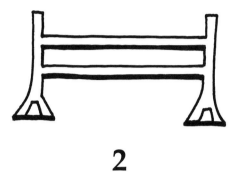

2

Tally watched as Ryan shook his head before addressing Mac. "Do it again. I want to see a Devon turn there."

Mac rolled her eyes but smiled at her trainer, who wasn't letting her get away with anything but an awesome turn at the end of their lesson.

"You got a great ribbon at one of the biggest horse shows in the country! It's all gonna be different from here on out, Mac. I'm holding you to a higher standard now." Ryan winked when he said that last bit, but that didn't mean he wasn't serious. Tally knew a lot of Ryan's little quirks now. A wink just meant he wasn't mad at you. You still needed to ride well and deliver.

Tally and Goose were done with their lesson for the day, having practiced several rollback turns themselves. Goose was still considerably less experienced than Mac's pony, Joey. So Ryan tended to end Goose's lessons on a positive note, not necessarily waiting for a perfect one. Drilling the same thing over and over on green ponies wasn't a productive training technique.

As Joey cantered past Goose on his way to the vertical, Tally noticed that his chestnut coat was a full shade darker with perspiration.

"Look early, Mac. If you've already landed when you turn your head, it's too late."

Mac (short for Mackenzie, like Tally was short for Natalia—one of the many things the girls discovered they had in common), turned her head a moment before Joey took off at the first fence. Then, she shaped a beautiful, tight turn to the oxer.

"Walk before the gate!" Ryan called out to them. Just a couple of strides out from the second jump, Mac slowed Joey to a walk, right in front of the gate. Tally recognized this as the way riders finished their handy courses at shows.

"*Ah ha*! See the difference when you look a stride sooner?"

Mac nodded and gave Joey a big pat.

"Good work today, both of you. Get those ponies nice and cool before you put them away."

Tally and Mac let Joey and G mosey around the pathway that connected the indoor and outdoor rings at the top of the hill to the wash stalls and barn down below. The Oaks barn was shaped like a horseshoe, with one aisle housing the lesson program's horses, and the other aisle devoted to boarders' horses. When Tally first started riding at Oaks, the boarders rode with several different trainers. But since Ryan's arrival last year, his business, Field Ridge, had taken over most of the boarder aisle. Oaks was happy to have him as their resident A Circuit hunter/jumper trainer, and most of the boarder stalls were now occupied by Field Ridge horses and ponies. A few other owners still kept their horses at the barn for pleasure and trail riding.

Mac shielded her eyes over the visor of her helmet and turned to Tally. "I feel like the sun is cooking these poor ponies. You want to walk another couple laps inside?"

Tally agreed and the pair walked into the smaller indoor ring between the two barn aisles. They chatted about their upcoming horse shows. Tally was getting more comfortable navigating the bigger shows off the property, while Mac was preparing for her next big milestone: Pony Finals, held every year in August. Both girls let their ponies stretch out to the buckle. A lesson was going to start in the small indoor shortly, and Tally watched a boy in half chaps and paddock boots talking to Brenna, the barn manager, in the bleachers.

Mac nodded her head toward him and gave Tally a quizzical look. They had reached the level of friendship where words became optional in certain conversations.

"I think he goes to my school," Tally said before swinging her leg over the saddle and hopping off of G. Mac dismounted too.

"I like when boys ride," Mac said cheerfully. "We have more than enough girls in this sport."

"Hey guys, go ahead and start trotting around," an instructor said from the middle of the ring. Tally and Mac turned and led the ponies out for a bath at the wash stalls.

3

With just a couple weeks left before summer break, everyone at Tally's middle school, Johnston West, felt antsy. It seemed like no one could sit still in classes, and the lunch room was louder and more boisterous than usual.

Tally's best friend from school, Kaitlyn Rowe, also took lessons at Oaks. Tally loved blending her two worlds together. Most of her school friends knew nothing about horses, and most of her barn friends, including Mac, went to other schools.

"What is wrong with seventh grade boys?" Kaitlyn asked with a huff, sitting down on the floor next to Tally. It was tradition for the seventh graders to sit on the floor in the cafeteria, something Tally thought was exceedingly dumb. Luckily, they'd be graduating to actual tables next year.

"What do you mean? Oh, hey, Ava," Tally said, greeting their other friend. Ava crossed one ankle in front of the other and sat down between her friends, all in one graceful motion. Ava used to ride but traded horses for gymnastics last Fall. Tally had always pined for a pony like Ava's, until she catch-rode him herself and found out he was a lot tougher than he looked.

"Ava, do you get made fun of for wearing your leotard?" Kaitlyn asked.

Ava wrinkled her nose as she

pulled a lunch bag out of her backpack.

"What do you mean?"

"I was reading a book about equitation before gym and those boys from our history class were neighing at me," Kaitlyn said.

Tally remembered the same thing happening to her at the beginning of the school year.

"They're so stupid," Ava said, rolling her eyes. "You know that sixth grader Jacob? He rides too, and the way they make fun of him is so horrible. I saw it during study hall one day. They say he's in a girls' sport and he shouldn't be a rider. They called him some awful names. Jacob didn't say anything back. I just felt so bad for him."

The bell rang and the girls said goodbye to one another before heading off to their next classes.

Tally felt a little guilty for being so upset about

having a boy neigh at her. Ava was right, it was stupid, and apparently it could be a whole lot worse. She thought back to the boy she saw talking to Brenna at the barn the other day. Was that Jacob from her school?

That afternoon, Tally had another shift on the school aisle. The barn manager, Brenna, had given her an unofficial working student position to earn a second lesson each week. Her parents provided the other. Tally never minded the extra work—she loved any time she got to spend around horses. Mucking stalls wasn't the most fun barn chore, of course, but it was well worth it.

"Do you ever get jealous of the kids who don't have to work for extra lessons?" Mac asked her recently. Mac had quickly become Tally's best friend at the barn, and they found they could talk about anything.

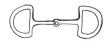

"I have before, yeah," Tally answered honestly. "But working for a lesson is no big deal. It's more about wishing I had a horse or a pony of my own and could show more often, you know? Like, that's a given for some kids. So, I guess I am a little jealous of that."

Mac nodded, her expression thoughtful.

"But my dad tells me that being jealous doesn't accomplish anything," Tally continued. "And, honestly, he's right. So, I try to focus on what I do have. And right now, I have a really cool pony to ride."

Tally arrived a little early for her shift that afternoon when school let out, so she ducked into the Field Ridge tack room first to wipe down her saddle. She and her parents had chipped in to buy it from an Oaks rider named Isabelle who'd grown too tall for it. Tally had never owned her own saddle before and took great pride in keeping it in pristine condition.

"Tal!" Ryan's booming voice had a way of crashing through the quiet on the boarder aisle. Tally stuck her head out of the tack room and gave him a wave.

"Hey, there you are," he said, walking toward her. "I want to give you and your parents a call in the next couple of days to talk about summer shows."

"Great," Tally said, feeling that now-familiar rush of horse show excitement. She and G had competed in just a couple of shows together thus far, but it felt like the pony was progressing super fast.

"I think Goose could be something really special, and could get sold as early as this August," Ryan

said. "We need to get more miles on him. Different places, different shows. What are your plans for the summer, anyway?"

"To ride."

Ryan laughed. "Well, good, that's what I was hoping for."

They hashed out some more details about the days that Tally would be working for Brenna, and Ryan said he'd call Tally's parents that night to talk about the shows. He had a few in mind that would put G in the best position to be sold as an eligible green. Ponies only had a year of eligibility for the green divisions, so the plan was to show Goose in the children's ponies so that when he got sold, he'd be able to compete in the small green division. All of this terminology had been new to Tally just a few months prior, but she followed everything Ryan was saying now. It was hard to keep from getting too attached to G, but she pushed the thought of him getting sold from her mind. Instead, she focused on making sure her mom and dad said yes to whatever shows Ryan wanted them to do.

But her parents surprised her that night.

"It sounds like you have a lot of competing to do this summer," Tally's dad said casually after dinner.

"You talked to Ryan already? It's a yes?"

Her mom smiled before answering. "It's a yes to the shows, but the only reason we're allowing so many is because it's almost summertime. During the school year, your education continues to come first. Got it?"

"I got it, yes. Thank you, thank you guys!" Tally felt like she could start crying, she was so excited. But with less than a week left of seventh grade,

school was the last thing on her mind. Her summer show season with G was about to begin, and their first stop would be a big equestrian complex an hour away.

4

Tally and G arrived at the Pinnacle Summer Classic on a Thursday after four days of rain. The weather had varied between drizzle and downpour, and all the water had wreaked havoc on the footing at the show complex. Each division that was scheduled to run in the two outdoor rings was either moved to the covered ring, the indoor, or taken off the show schedule altogether. Suddenly, G's third horse show would also be his first time showing indoors away from home.

The night before shipping out, Tally and Mac had watched their ponies trot around and play in the small indoor. Ryan wanted them to have some turnout to stretch their legs, but going out in the fields was not an option, as the paddocks had practically turned into lakes.

"Is it going to be a lot spookier for him, showing in the indoor at Pinnacle?" Tally asked Mac.

"Well, any time they're away from home it's spookier, indoor or not," Mac began. Tally loved having a friend who would happily answer all her horse show questions. "But yeah, the lights in an indoor are going to make it spookier than it would be outside. And the indoor at Pinnacle has stadium seating, so, depending on how close people are sitting, Goose may have a lot to look at in the stands, too."

Tally exhaled slowly, feeling her show nerves kick in early. "Thanks, Mac, that's very reassuring."

"Hey, I'm just being honest with you! But don't worry. Ryan won't put G in a situation he can't handle. Your classes are definitely in the indoor?"

Tally nodded.

"That's too bad. The covered ring, once you're in it, isn't really any scarier than the outdoor rings for most ponies."

"That's super nice for people showing in that one," Tally said dryly, and Mac swatted Tally's arm with her baseball cap.

The girls watched as Joey bucked down the long side of the ring. At the other end, G sniffed a mounting block before prancing away and whinnying.

Tally smiled. "I think the ponies are excited, too."

As she was putting some things away in the

Field Ridge tack room before leaving the barn that evening, Tally noticed that someone had changed the quote of the day on the white board. It now read: "You don't always need a plan. Sometimes you need to breathe, trust, let go, and just see what happens."

Tally paused to think about the quote. It sounded like the way Ryan described trusting a horse or pony's canter to get her to the jumps just right. But it also applied to the bigger picture. She knew she was falling in love with a sales pony, so it was a love affair that wouldn't end happily for her. What would come next? Tally had no choice but to follow the advice scribbled on the white board: to trust, let go, and just see what happens.

The next morning, Mac's mom drove both girls to the Pinnacle Summer Classic. The showgrounds had around two hundred permanent stalls, which

Mac said was more comfortable for the animals than the temporary tent-stall setups at many of the other shows. Field Ridge's head groom, Lupe, had both ponies already waiting for the girls in the indoor, which was open for schooling that morning. Tally and Mac arrived dressed and ready to ride.

A constant, low whine over the PA system was the first thing Tally noticed in the indoor. She hoped it wouldn't be too distracting for G, who was looking in every direction around the ring while Tally walked a lap. She had to keep her own head on a swivel too, in order to avoid any oncoming ponies.

"Mac and Tally, pick up your trot. Mac, you work on bending for six strides, then ride straight for six strides, then counter bend for six strides. Repeat that a couple of times. Tally, make circles in each of the corners to keep the pony's attention on you and not

what's going on in the ring."

G felt light and springy underneath her, and Tally was pleased to find that she was able to keep his attention relatively easily. The pony had an unusual backstory. He was born in someone's backyard—they didn't even know their mare was pregnant—and was started slowly at another barn, where he stayed for two years before coming to Field Ridge. Through weeks of lessons with Tally and some tune-up rides by Isabelle, G was really "getting with the program," as her trainer put it, performing well at home and at the few shows they'd done away.

When the girls were done flatting, Ryan set some low verticals in the ring. Unlike in a schooling area with a couple of plain jumps, the actual show jumps were already set in the ring, and competitors were permitted to school over them.

"Everything is just topsy-turvy with the weather," Ryan explained. "But let's take advantage of getting this chance to show Goose the jumps under the lights."

They cantered up to their first fence, which had fancy, swirly standards and a row of colorful flowerboxes under the rail; Tally didn't know what G might do.

"Put that leg on, Tally, don't just sit there!" Ryan said. "You need to be definitive here, and give this pony some confidence."

G cantered all the way to the base of the jump and popped over it, cracking his back to make an exaggeratedly round effort. It jumped Tally loose, and she scrambled to regain her stirrups as they cantered away.

"More leg this time, get up to that ring pace, and

you'll catch it right out of stride. Do it again."

Ring pace, Tally repeated to herself, thinking back on their lessons. She needed more canter, and G was happy to deliver. The next time they got to the vertical, they found a more comfortable take-off spot and G jumped the fence with considerably less drama.

"Better! Now come around and catch this diagonal line in seven strides."

For just a stride or two, Tally felt her whole body go slack from nerves before putting her leg back on. She tried focusing entirely on the canter, rather than thinking about what the jumps looked like, or what G might think of them. The strategy paid off, and they cantered down the line in seven strides without any theatrics from the pony.

"Ah ha! See what happens when you give him

the confidence? You guys are starting to trust each other." Ryan called both ponies and riders in to the center of the ring before having them dismount and walk to barn six, the ponies' temporary home for the show week.

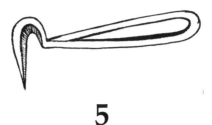

5

"Remember that guy we saw at Oaks talking to Brenna in the bleachers?" Mac asked Tally early the next morning as they tacked their ponies up for schooling in the indoor. "Well he's here and I think he's trailering in to ride with Ryan."

"What's trailering in?" Tally asked as she threaded G's noseband through his martingale.

"It's when you keep your horse at home or at another barn, and you trailer them in for lessons or horse shows. I just saw our guy heading for the indoor. Maybe we're all going to ride together."

When Tally and G got to the ring with the other ponies, the boy was cantering down the long side on his horse, a small bay gelding with a stocky build. The horse's mane was unbraided, and the boy's saddle was situated on top of a square saddle pad, rather than the shaped ones Tally had become accustomed to in the pony hunter divisions.

"More leg, Jacob, keep building up that canter and come hop over this single here."

So it *was* the boy from her school, Tally realized. Jacob had great posture and presence in the saddle and enviably deep heels. His horse was cute too, and on the smaller side like Sweetie, Tally's favorite school horse. They popped over the single and as they cantered away, Ryan raised the top rail by a couple of holes.

"Come get it again, Jacob," he called.

Tally walked G around the ring and listened as the announcer told everyone that there would be just twenty more minutes for schooling before the first division began.

"Tally and Mac, you guys trot around and then we'll jump these ponies a little."

Their schooling ride went by in a blur for Tally, who was probably more distracted by all the activity than the pony. Schooling in the indoor was an unusual setup, but a necessary one, since the outdoor schooling areas were in such bad shape. Everyone was trying to squeeze in some jumping in the indoor show ring before the first division was set to begin.

Ryan called his three riders over to one corner, safely out of the way from all the traffic.

"Bit of a zoo here today, guys, so I'm going to lean on Lupe to help everyone get where they need to be. Please stay in touch with him so you're in the right spot and on time. Jacob, have you met these guys yet?"

Jacob shook his head no, but smiled.

"Jacob just started trailering in for lessons with me, and this is his horse, Carlo. Jacob, this is Tally and Goose, he's one of our sales ponies. And this is Mac and her pony, Joey."

"Nice to meet you all," Jacob said.

"Okay, I've got a couple kids going in the covered ring, so I'll be over there. You guys let your ponies chill out in their stalls for a bit and I'll see you soon."

Everyone followed Ryan up the ramp that lead from the indoor ring to the show grounds. At the top, Ryan went to the right, where a row of trainers' golf carts were parked. The riders went left, toward their barn.

"How's it going?" Mac asked Jacob as they walked.

"It's going okay, how about you guys?"

"Good," Tally chimed in. "You go to Johnston West, right?"

"I thought I recognized you! You're going into eighth grade?"

"Yeah," said Tally. "What do you show Carlo in?"

"I think we're moving up to the low children's jumpers at this show," Jacob said thoughtfully. "But my mom and I are a little unsure about the right division for Carlo."

"Ryan is really good about finding the right spot for horses," said Mac. "How are you liking riding with him so far?"

"I like him a lot," Jacob said, his tone serious. "My mom and I have always had horses on our property. I rode with this one trainer near our house for a while, but we heard such good things about Ryan. He's tough!"

"He really is," Tally and Mac answered in unison, laughing at their synchronicity. "But you'll learn a lot from him," Mac added.

Jacob nodded. "I can tell. Well, my mom is over there with the trailer so I'm gonna go untack and let Carlo eat a little bit. See you later?"

"See ya!" Tally said as the girls stopped their ponies in front of barn six.

"He seems nice," Mac said as she slid to the ground, careful to avoid Joey's braids on the way down.

"I heard he gets bullied in school for riding."

"Bullied for riding? Why?" Mac looked incredulous.

"I guess the other guys in his grade

think it's a girls' sport."

"That's so dumb," Mac said as Lupe appeared and helped with the ponies. "Look at the top show jumpers! And even the big eq. There's so many guys in the sport."

"How did he school?" Lupe asked, gesturing to Joey. Tally had been noticing that Lupe took great interest in their riding. It made her feel so good to be part of a team.

"Good, thanks!" Mac replied as Lupe walked Joey to his stall. "He likes this ring, I think."

Lupe replied with a double thumbs-up. "You girls go out and crush 'em today!"

6

With clients showing in two rings—a golf cart's ride apart from each other—Ryan really did lean on Lupe's help more than usual. Once Tally was back at the ring with Goose, Ryan delivered an unsettling message to her through Lupe.

"Tally, you're going to go first in the children's ponies," Lupe told Tally as she went over the course in her mind.

"Wait, you mean first? Like, I don't even get to watch another pony go?" Tally felt her heart starting to thud with nervous energy.

"Psst!" Mac said from the ground in an exaggerated whisper. "You don't need to watch anyone go. It's single, outside, diagonal, outside."

The announcer was pinning the class before hers, and there would be no break to reset the jumps. Tally gazed at the jumps in the ring for a few minutes, thinking about steadying her breathing and riding the same way she did in lessons.

"Ready, Tal?" Ryan asked, suddenly right next to her.

"I guess," Tally said, as the ring starter nodded at her to go in. It wasn't until they were on their approach to the single that Tally realized the hurry to get in for her trip prevented her from having time to be nervous. They cleared the first jump, a single vertical on the diagonal, before she could give any more thought to going first.

Goose popped an easy lead change well before the corner, and Tally realized that he was relaxed because she was. Not that this was some news flash; that's how animals fed off their rider's energy, but it was exciting to notice it happening in real time.

I'm just gonna go with this, Tally thought as they approached the outside line. Instead of her usual mental chatter, Tally focused on keeping her leg on and enjoying a newfound sense of confidence. About four strides out, she felt Goose start to raise his head—his usual move if he was then going to peek at a jump—so Tally closed her leg tighter. He instantly relaxed, dropped his head, and jumped the vertical without looking down or swapping.

Huh! Tally thought, barely able to contain her smile. Could it really be this easy?

Goose made a nice effort over the oxer out of the line. Tally pulled her shoulders back and put her leg on as they passed the in-gate. It was like the pony was in the zone as much as she was.

Tally steered G to the diagonal line, closing her fingers on the reins when he got a little strong, backing it up with her leg so he wouldn't break to the trot. He came back to her, jumping in quietly. Tally opened his stride just a bit to the oxer in order to get the correct number of strides. It almost felt invisible. Landing off the diagonal, G leaned to the inside, and Tally felt her mental chatter starting up again, but when she shifted her weight to the outside and redirected G off his forehand, he got a nice, clean change. They cantered the outside line, coming home like they'd both been showing in big indoors their whole lives.

After they landed off the final jump, Ryan whistled at the in-gate and Mac cheered loudly.

"That was a brilliant ride," Ryan said when Tally came out. "I should throw you in first more often."

"I honestly think that it helped," Tally said as she caught her breath. "It was just fun and I stopped thinking so hard."

"Good! Now go do that again," Ryan said, giving G a big pat and feeding him a peppermint.

Tally had one more trip for the day in her division and it was similar to the first. It was like she'd unlocked some sort of riding secret to feeling more and thinking less. Replicating it at future shows—or even in the rest of her division tomorrow—would be another matter, of course. But for now, she basked in the glow of a horse show where everything just clicked.

Ryan rushed back to the covered ring to help Jacob in his jumper division next. When Lupe offered to take G back to his stall, Tally gratefully accepted. She hated not getting to cool the pony out herself, but she wanted to support her new barn friend, particularly in light of what she'd heard about him being bullied at school.

"You want to come watch Jacob with me, Mac?"

"I wish I could, but I have to go get ready. I may run out of time going back and forth between the rings, you know?"

"No problem," Tally said, and turned to leave but her friend held a hand up.

"What?" Tally asked.

"Hang on a second," whispered Mac, her head cocked to the side, like she was listening to something. Then she shook her head in disgust.

"You know, sometimes I really don't like horse show people."

"What do you mean?"

"Those girls over there were talking about you. How you've got your hair up and tall boots on a small pony," Mac said, rolling her eyes.

"Is that bad?" Tally's excitement over their two great trips quickly blended with self-consciousness.

"Of course not. It's usually older, more experienced riders who are on green ponies like this, bringing them along. You're fine. Ignore them."

For all the quiet in Tally's mind while she was in the ring, her head was now flooded with thoughts about which girls were talking about her. Should she be in paddock boots like the other pony riders?

"Hey," Mac interjected, smiling. "You know they wouldn't be saying anything if you didn't ride so

well, right? Those trips are going to be tough to beat, Tally. And you're the one making up this pony! That is nothing but jealousy right there."

Mac left for the barn while Tally started the long walk to the covered ring. As her boots squished in the muddy ground. Tally was surprised to find herself smiling. Mac was right. Those girls were talking about her because she'd ridden so well. Tally decided she wasn't going to care that much what people might say about her. Let them talk.

7

Jacob was already in the ring by the time Tally arrived. Ryan was watching him at the in-gate. Both of them looked nervous.

"In for their power and speed class, this is number 520, Jacob Viston, riding Carlo."

Tally thought it would be obvious to just about anyone how great Jacob looked on a horse. Jacob's position was so solid, with a tight lower leg and deep heels, that Tally almost didn't notice the bit of awkwardness Carlo had to his jumping style.

As they rounded a corner to the in-and-out, Carlo held his head high and Jacob sat deeply in the saddle, turning his toes out slightly to use his spurs on the little bay.

Carlo rubbed the vertical jumping in and took an abbreviated stride in the middle. There was a moment of hesitation—Tally wasn't sure if he'd take off long after one stride or try to squeeze in a second—and Jacob clucked at his horse. The gelding took off after one stride, but he didn't have the step or the scope to clear the oxer. He punched out the top rail hard, and when he put his front legs down to land the jump, one hoof came down squarely on top of the fallen rail. Carlo stumbled, and Jacob came down on his neck in a heap. The pair scrambled away, and Jacob pulled the horse up swiftly. Carlo was limping.

"The rider is excused, thank you," said the announcer.

Was that really necessary? Tally thought, her face burning for her new barn friend and her heart breaking for his horse.

Ryan jogged into the ring and ran up Carlo's stirrups, his eyes carefully trained on the horse's front legs as they walked out of the ring.

Tally kept her distance as Ryan checked out Carlo's right front leg, calling a vet to come look as well. Jacob's mom joined them, and the group talked among themselves until Jacob walked toward Tally, his head down.

"Hey," Tally said, and Jacob looked up at her. He was trying not to cry.

"Hey."

"What did the vet say?" Tally asked.

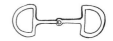

"She doesn't think it's serious, but there's no way to know for sure yet. We just have to let him rest."

Jacob's mom motioned for him to come over to the group. Jacob gave Tally a little wave before heading back to his horse.

Tally hurried back toward the indoor to catch Mac's trips, but when she got inside, her friend was dismounting.

"Tal! Is everything okay? Ryan said there was an emergency, so he had another trainer help me here."

"Jacob's horse crashed through the in-and-out and he's hurt. The vet doesn't think it's serious but there's no way to know for sure yet," Tally said.

Mac nodded solemnly. There was always the risk of a horse or rider getting hurt in their sport, but it was never easy when it actually happened.

"Did I miss your trips?" Tally asked.

"Yeah. But that's okay, I understand. Did you get to talk to Jacob?"

Tally nodded her head. "He was upset but really focused on his horse. How was Joey?"

"Good," Mac said, patting his neck. "Really solid, no big mistakes. And most importantly, no chipping! After this show, I think we just have one more before Pony Finals."

The girls and Lupe walked back toward the barn. Mac suggested checking the results on a website that updated them in real time. Tally was delighted to learn that Goose won both of the children's classes out of a dozen ponies; Mac was second and third in an even bigger medium pony division.

"Let's go collect our loot," Mac said after they'd checked water and feed buckets for both ponies at the barn.

Just then, both girls heard some commotion outside.

"You go that way and I'll wait here in case she comes back," someone said.

"Does anyone have some grain handy?"

"Loose pony!"

Four people spread out to catch a little black pony with a white blaze who looked quite pleased to be playing hide and seek.

"Luna!" one woman with a bucket of grain called to the pony. When she got within ten paces, though, Luna dropped her head and turned on her hind end, prancing away.

"She does this at every show," a rider in boots just as muddy as Tally's said to her with a laugh.

"Wait, the pony always gets loose?"

"Yep," the girl said, nodding her head. "She's

great in the show ring, but the minute her kid takes the bridle off and doesn't have control, Luna goes on a tour of the show grounds. She tries all the grass. It's pretty funny at this point because we know we'll always catch her."

"Luna bear!" someone else called to the pony, who was now sniffing around barn six.

Tally giggled. She still felt a little preoccupied, thinking about Jacob, but there was something just so silly and charming about a pony who regularly got loose like this. She turned toward Mac and smiled.

"Never know what you're going to get at a show, huh?"

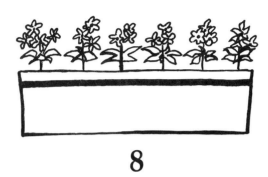

8

A couple days after returning home from the Pinnacle Summer Classic, Tally was moving flower boxes into the show office when she saw Jacob walking toward the ring with Sweetie.

He smiled upon seeing a familiar face.

"How's Carlo?" Tally asked.

"He's on stall rest for a while. But it could have been a lot worse, so I'm relieved," Jacob said, petting Sweetie's shoulder.

"So glad to hear that," Tally said, setting a flower

box down and brushing the dirt off her hands. "You're going to lesson on Sweetie? She's the best."

"Yeah, I've heard she's a lot of fun. I'm glad I can keep riding with Ryan while Carlo gets better. Hey, how did you and Mac end up doing at the show?"

"Really well, actually," Tally said. "Goose was champion in the children's ponies, and Joey was reserve in the mediums."

"Wow, that's awesome, congrats!"

"Thanks," Tally said. "I'm proud of that little guy. Have a great lesson."

For the next fifteen minutes, Tally walked back and forth moving flower boxes and walls. When a rider in another lesson started jumping a course, Ryan asked Jacob to halt Sweetie near his director's chair in the center of the ring. Tally stood with them too, to stay out of the way.

"Your mom said Carlo's on the mend. I'm glad to hear it," Ryan said to Jacob.

"Thanks, so am I," Jacob said.

"I'm sorry to tell you this, but I think the one-meter classes are outside of Carlo's scope. You'd serve him better to be really successful at a lower height," said Ryan. Tally felt a bit awkward overhearing this conversation but made a mental note to look up how big one-meter fences were.

"I agree. I think my old trainer was so focused on us moving up that . . . I don't know. I wish I'd realized sooner that Carlo was overmatched."

"Don't worry about that," Ryan said. "We're going to do right by Carlo now. Some trainers are too preoccupied with their clients moving up, if you ask me. Later on, if you're ready to move up to the meter classes and Carlo is not, then we can have another conversation about a horse that's more suited to where you want to go. But for now, let's keep you in the saddle, and when Carlo recovers, you guys can go kill it together in the point-eight meter. How's that sound?"

"Great," Jacob replied with a big grin, looking relieved.

Tally watched the rest of his lesson while she worked in the larger indoor, noting how happy Sweetie looked with Jacob. She couldn't ignore the pang of jealousy over someone new riding her favorite school horse—and riding the mare so well—but, as Ryan pointed out, doing right by the horses was the important part of their sport. She was happy that Sweetie was happy.

After Tally's shift concluded that afternoon, she and Mac had plans to visit a tack store with a larger

selection than the one on the Oaks property. Mac needed a new show coat.

Riding in the back of Mac's mom's car, the girls discussed how Jacob would be stepping down a division or two once Carlo was healed.

"I've heard about that other trainer," Mac said in a low voice. "She can be a little…reckless. Have you heard of the phrase 'turn and burn'?"

Tally shook her head no.

"If you watch enough jumper classes you'll see what I mean. Ryan was smart to have them go down to the point-eight meter. That way, Carlo will be more confident, and stay healthy, too."

"That lady doesn't sound like a very good trainer, but it also seems to me like horse show people talk. Like, a lot," Tally said.

"Tal, you are so cute," Mac said, laughing.

"What?"

"It's just so true, what you said. Kinda fun to see these lightbulb moments happening for you."

"I know it's not a big deal, but I'm still surprised that people were talking about how I wore tall boots on a small pony," Tally said.

"It's stupid how much people talk, but you're doing the right thing. You're tall and you're comfortable in tall boots, so who cares what people think? Ryan will tell you if he wants to change anything, trust me. You're fine," Mac said with a confident nod.

"Almost there, girls," Mac's mom announced. Her daughter let out a little squeal of excitement.

"I love when I get to combine my two passions," she said to Tally with a wink. "Riding and shopping!"

9

The grassy stretch outside the tack shop was dotted with kid-sized jumps in all shapes and colors. Mac made a beeline for them. Tally liked wedging wrapping paper tubes in the doorways at her house to jump, but this was a far fancier setup. Standards, rails, walls, and flower boxes were designed exactly like hunter and jumper fences, just scaled down to kidsize.

"Hop on," Mac said, grinning at Tally and bending down, standard positioning for a piggyback ride. Tally giggled and jumped up as softly as she could.

Mac caught Tally behind the knees and cantered off to a red-and-white vertical.

Tally laughed at her friend as Mac came to an almost complete stop before hiking her legs up over the little jump.

"Points off for style," Tally joked and jumped down. Mac bent over, hands on her knees.

"That was so much harder than I thought it would be!" Mac said between breaths. Then she stood up straight and cantered a couple of the fences, riderless.

"Much better," Tally said. "Eighty-five."

The girls and Mac's mom made their way inside, the store's air-conditioning providing a shocking contrast from the muggy summer afternoon.

"Can I help you ladies with anything?" asked a store employee, just as they started browsing the show coats.

"My daughter outgrew her last show jacket, so we're looking for a new one," Mac's mom said, turning briefly to her daughter. "Your shadbelly still fits, right?"

Mac nodded. "Yeah, Isabelle gave it to me. It's actually a little big still, but Ryan said it's fine. I think it'll fit for a while."

"Until the next growth spurt anyway, right?" Mac's mom said to the employee, a teenage girl who was dressed in a college sweatshirt and breeches.

"So it goes!" said the girl before asking Mac for her size and pulling some options.

"I'm going to go look at the model horses," Mac's mom said, walking toward another corner of the store. "I have to buy a gift for your cousin, Mackenzie. Just come get me when you find a jacket you like."

As Mac tried on coats, Tally glanced around the

store, laughing at a red octagon-shaped sign that read WHOA instead of STOP.

"We should get Ryan to buy that for the barn," Tally said to Mac, who was sizing up a navy blue coat.

"I don't love the fit of this one," the salesgirl said. "Why don't I pull you a few four-button styles? They're just as acceptable in the hunter and equitation rings as the three-button. They can be more flattering, too, if you're a little fuller around the midsection. I'll be right back."

As the girl walked away, Tally nudged her friend.

"What, do you not get it or something? It says WHOA instead of STOP. I think we need it for the Oaks driveway." But Mac looked completely distracted, like she didn't even hear what Tally was saying.

"Did you hear what that girl just said?"

"No, what?" asked Tally.

"She said four-button jackets are more flattering if you're fuller." Mac looked like she might start crying.

"So? She wasn't talking about you being 'fuller.'"

"I think she was," Mac said, looking down at her boots. "Okay! Here's what I've got in the four-button," the salesgirl said, returning with an armful of navy and black coats.

Mac changed her expression the same way Tally had seen her do in the show ring. She looked determined and unbothered as the girl helped her into several show jackets. She turned around in the mirror a few times when she found one she liked.

"Will you go get my mom? I think I want to get this one," Mac said.

When Tally returned with Mac's mom, the store employee told them that the sleeves were a bit long so that Mac would get more wear out of the jacket, rather than if they bought one size smaller.

"Okay, as long as you don't think the sleeves are too long," Mac's mom said.

"I don't think they are. I know Ryan and I think he'll be okay with the fit, too. But if I'm wrong you can definitely bring it back and we'll exchange it for a size down."

The group proceeded to the register where Mac's mom paid for the coat. Mac appeared to have forgotten about the salesgirl's comment. At least, Tally hoped she had.

The next day at the barn, while she was working on the school aisle, Tally found Jacob in Sweetie's stall.

"Hey! You guys looked great together in your lesson the other day. Do you like Sweetie?"

"I do. She's . . . well, she's a sweetie," Jacob said with a little laugh.

"She is," Tally said, digging in her jeans pocket and unwrapping a peppermint for the mare. "How's Carlo doing?"

"A lot better, actually, thanks for asking."

"Oh, good!" Tally said.

Jacob was absentmindedly braiding Sweetie's forelock as they talked. The mare didn't seem to mind in the slightest.

"When we jogged him for the vet he looked sound, so that's good. I think we'll trailer in for a lesson within a week or two."

"Awesome!" Tally said.

"Thanks. Hey, this may be weird to say, but I just wanted to, um. . .thank you," Jacob said, dropping Sweetie's forelock and adjusting the pockets on his breeches.

"Thank me for what?" Tally asked.

"For being so nice to me. That sounds really lame, doesn't it? But I get made fun of at school all the time. So it's nice to know that everyone at Johnston West isn't a jerk."

"That's awful," Tally said. "Guys at school neigh at me and Kaitlyn but I'm sure it's worse when you're a boy."

"It's really hard," Jacob said, taking a deep breath. "Guys at school say I shouldn't ride because it's a girls' sport. A lot of guys at school will say, 'Oh you're gay,' or, 'You're a sissy for riding horses. Do a real sport.'"

Tally felt startled by what Jacob said. It was definitely far worse than the occasional neigh she got from boys at school.

"They have no idea how much of a real sport riding is," Tally said softly.

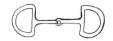

"Yeah," Jacob added with the hint of a smile. "I'd like to see one of them ride a pony that's stopping, or a horse who decides to buck."

"We should invite them out to try," Tally deadpanned. And Jacob smiled for real.

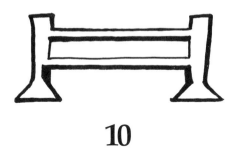

10

"I'm here, sweet boy!"

A few days later Tally practically jogged down the Field Ridge aisle to see Goose. He walked over to the stall guard across his doorway and stretched his head out toward her. Goose turned his head diagonally, which always made Tally laugh.

"Is that how you say hello?" she asked him, still giggling.

"He's so cute. He really loves you," Isabelle said from the end of the aisle.

"Aw, thanks," Tally replied. "The feeling is definitely mutual!"

Before her lesson, Tally groomed Goose on the cross ties, scratching his favorite spots as she went.

"Be right back, buddy," she said. The pony fixed his ears on her while she ducked into the tack room.

"Oh!" Tally practically tripped over Mac, who was seated on her trunk just inside the doorway. "Sorry, I didn't see you there!" When Mac lifted her face, Tally saw that it was red and tear-stained.

"Mac, what's wrong?"

Mac pulled at her tank top, looking uncomfortable. "This," she said, gesturing to her midsection. "I'm 'fuller,' don't you remember?"

"Mac. . ." Tally began, but her friend held up her hand.

"I had to get new breeches, too.

Nothing fits me anymore."

"You're growing," Tally offered, but it didn't seem to help. Then, Isabelle popped into the tack room.

"Oh no! What happened?"

Tally filled her in on the tack store encounter, and Isabelle sat down on the floor in front of Mac's trunk.

"Look, there's a lot of judgment in this sport, everywhere you go," Isabelle said. "People are constantly judging each other. It's the worst."

"Remember the girls talking about me being too big on G?" Tally said. "And I was just talking to Jacob the other day about how guys at our school tease him for being a rider."

"That's terrible," Isabelle said, looking solemn. "For us, it happens from within the sport, too, right? It's really uncool for a tack store employee to say something like that. We should be encouraging each

other. But I know just how you feel, Mac. I'm built like an athlete, too, not like an equitation princess. I've always been more strong than skinny. I hated that in middle school but now I'm okay with it. Strong is great. Really."

Mac sniffled again and looked thoughtful. "I've just been feeling lately like I must be fat, you know? I didn't think about it like, maybe I'm just strong rather than skinny."

"Exactly. You look like an athlete and that's awesome. And, hello, you're twelve—you should be getting new show coats and breeches all the time until you're done growing. And just so you know, lots of girls do well in the equitation even if they don't have the tall and skinny look that everyone thinks is so important. It's not."

"Come on," Tally said, helping her friend up from

the tack trunk. "If you don't have Joey ready for our lesson on time, Ryan is going to have you crying for a whole other reason."

Up in the large indoor, the girls and their ponies got into the rhythm of bending and working laterally on the flat. Jacob was on Sweetie in their lesson, too. Thinking about how upset Mac was, Tally was glad that being kind to Jacob could make a difference for him after all the bullying.

"Be sure you're giving with your hands, Jacob. Better. Tally, you too, less of a stranglehold on that outside rein, huh? Mac, I got nothin' right now. Keep on keepin' on."

The group moved from their flatwork into cantering a bending line of ground rails in seven strides, then six, then five. Tally loved exercises like this, especially when Goose responded so well to

her aids, extending and compressing his big stride. Then Ryan set up standards for all of the rails so each was set as a low vertical. Both ponies did well cantering the five and six strides, but Tally found she really needed to change her track to get the seven done, now that they were little jumps instead of just ground rails.

On their first attempt at the seven strides, G got a little bit lost, thinking Tally was steering him away from the second jump of the bending line. She had to awkwardly steer him back to the track, taking off quite long after seven strides on their first attempt.

"Took a bit tour there!" Ryan said with a good-natured laugh. "Now we see his greenness a little, huh?"

"Yeah, I was so focused on changing the track, I think I accidentally convinced him we were going back to the rail," Tally said.

"That's okay! Try it again and this time keep your eye on the second jump in the air over the first. Keep the pony bent to the inside a bit so he knows where he's going."

Their next attempt was far smoother, with G proving himself to be a quick study yet again. The moment Tally set her eyes on the second jump of the bending line, she felt G lock onto it as well. Keeping a slight bend to the inside, even as she rode the wider track, prevented any confusion about where they were going.

"Beautiful!" Ryan called out. "Do it one more time in five now. Open up his stride a little on the long side, then when you make the turn, look for your inside track."

Tally asked Goose for a slightly more open canter

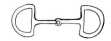

and then turned sooner, looking for a track that would get them there in an easy five strides.

Ryan had raised both verticals when she wasn't looking.

"Keep the ride the same," he said calmly, and she took a breath. No need to change the ride just for a few holes up.

G rounded his back nicely up over the first vertical, and Tally sat back into the saddle for their settled five strides. He jumped out quiet and round.

"Nailed it! Well done, Tal. Walk a lap, and then hop off a minute."

When Tally dismounted in the center, she was surprised to find a little girl in full chaps standing next to Ryan.

"This is Hazel," Ryan said, gesturing to the girl. "She's in my next lesson today, and I'd like her to hop on Goose. Let's see how he does with someone a little less experienced on his back."

"Cool," Tally replied, genuinely interested in seeing how G would go with another rider. Of course, this was the first step toward him getting sold, but for now, Tally enjoyed a proud pony-mama moment.

Goose stood perfectly still and polite while the little rider mounted. She was a good fit for a small pony.

"He's all warmed up, so just walk half a lap, stretching down through your heels, and then pick up your posting trot," Ryan said to Hazel before turning to Tally. "Time to see if our work has paid off!"

Tally immediately felt nervous.

"Don't be nervous," Ryan said, showing off his ability to practically read her mind—or at least her body language.

When Hazel picked up a trot on G, he looked happy as could be.

"A little more trot than that, Hazel," Ryan called. "I don't know how many kids got on this pony before you," he added to Tally. "What we're looking for here, essentially, is how appropriate he is for children. Smaller children, I mean, who haven't got the mileage that you've got."

Tally couldn't help breaking out in a ridiculous grin. She had mileage now. That was something to be pumped about.

Ryan and Tally watched as Goose trotted and cantered around, popping up over a couple cross rails and small verticals. Goose looked like he did this every day, packing around a little rider.

"I'm really proud of you both, Tal," Ryan said as Hazel walked the pony out. "So far so good with our guy. And you've got something special too, kiddo. Riding different ponies, particularly green ones, you need an innate sense about when to be soft and when to be tough. You've got that in spades. It's natural for you. Even when Goose does sell, my plan is to have you keep riding the sales guys for me. If that works for you, of course."

"Absolutely. Thank you, Ryan!" Tally was thrilled by the prospect of more catch-riding. However, her feelings of excitement were tinged with a deep sadness over the thought of never seeing Goose again.

11

"We won the classic?" Lupe asked Mac on a humid July afternoon. The Field Ridge team had arrived that morning for another horse show at the private school showgrounds near Oaks. Mac and Joey's division had gone early, culminating in the pony hunter classic.

"We just barely won, because Joey is perfect," Mac said with a laugh. She and Lupe exchanged high fives.

Tally smiled at her friend, happy for her to have

finished on such a high note before she would head to Kentucky for Pony Finals. Mac was determined not to let the nerves get to her like they did at Devon back in the spring. When it was time to leave for Kentucky, she said, it was going to be all about having fun. Still, Tally thought, winning the pony hunter classic a few weeks before Pony Finals could only help!

"Oh, and I brought these for you," Lupe added, presenting a pair of polo wraps to Mac.

"I thought I lost these! I'm so happy, where did you find them?" Mac asked him.

"Didn't I tell you? I brought them home for my mother to reattach the Velcro with her sewing machine."

"Wow, thank you so much," said Mac.

"That is just so cool," Tally said, nodding in Lupe's

direction. "I love our barn family."

Tally watched the small pony division finish up in the big outdoor ring, and listened in on the conversations around her.

"You're looking down. Stop pulling on him and go!" one trainer said as her rider on course passed the in-gate. The rider had an earlier stop in her medal trip, but was doing so much better now. Still, she never cracked a smile, on course or afterward. The ribbons on the ends of her braids fluttered and bounced above her as she finished off an impressive course. The next pony rider to enter the course had braces, Tally noticed, and a huge grin. Such a range of emotions on a horse show day, she thought. Tally watched the next trainer step up to the in-gate, the universal horse show claiming of a rider.

"Don't look your pony in the eye; look ahead

when you jog," another trainer said to her tiny rider, who was holding the reins of a sweet-looking bay pony.

"When is your division, Tal? Do we have time to try and watch Jacob?" Mac asked, tucking her gloves and helmet into her horse show backpack.

"There's one more division before mine starts, plus they have to reset the jumps, so I think we have time," Tally said.

"Great. The jumpers are in ring three, so let's head over."

The girls watched a couple of riders go before it was Jacob's turn. Their new barn friend exchanged some words with Ryan, who stood at the in-gate, before calmly entering the ring to await the buzzer. When it went off, Carlo sprung into an animated canter.

"I meant to ask you, how big are the jumps in one-meter classes?" Tally asked.

"A meter is three-foot-three," Mac said.

"Oh wow, that's bigger than I thought. What's this class?"

"I think this is point-eight meters," Mac said. "It comes out around two-foot-six."

The girls watched as Jacob steered Carlo to an oxer and the horse cleared it easily. Both of them looked happy, too, Tally thought with a sense of relief.

"And our rider is clear through the first round," the announcer said. "Rider is clear."

Tally watched as Jacob slowed Carlo to a trot and then a walk, the little bay gelding holding his head high and proud. Jacob glanced around the ring, turning to say something to Ryan, and the buzzer sounded again.

"What's he doing?" Tally asked.

"The jump-off," Mac said.

"Wait! He has to jump the first course and then the jump-off right after it? Like, remembering them both at the same time?" Tally could hardly believe it. She'd never stress about memorizing a medal course ever again.

"Yep." Mac nodded. "I could never do the jumpers!"

The jump-off had seven fences and the pair handily cleared them all. The announcer declared the round clear and Jacob smiled more broadly than Tally had seen to date. Ryan reached up to give Jacob a high five and to give Carlo a pat.

"Well done, Jacob, you rode that just right," Ryan said. It was hard not to hear Ryan when he used his

default volume. You could sometimes hear him from an entire show ring away. "Let's stick with this ride today, make sure the horse stays sound, and then we'll have a little fun with the turn options next time. Or even do the point-nine meter. But we'll keep him somewhere that he can really shine, huh?"

Jacob nodded his head before walking toward the girls, both of whom added their congrats when he dismounted.

"You guys looked great!" Mac said, giving Carlo a rub on his neck.

"Thanks. I'm just so glad he's okay. Ryan was right—our old trainer shouldn't have pushed us to the meter classes just for the sake of moving to the next division. Carlo is awesome and he's really going to kill it with the fences a little smaller, you know? It's not always about moving up."

"Hey, kids," Lupe said, walking up next to Tally. "Tally-o, time to go."

Tally waited for the usual rush of anticipation and nerves, but they never came. She waited for the butterflies at the in-gate, but nothing. She expected them while cantering to the first fence, but nada. This is a really cool new horse show development, she thought to herself before turning her attention back to the course.

Goose had one swap in front of an oxer, and he was late on a lead change, but otherwise their first trip was solid. The second two trips were much the same. Tally kept glancing down at G's braids and her own polished boots, almost trying to incite the show nerves, since it felt strange without them. But it didn't work. This was just part of what she did now, showing a braided pony in her shiny tall boots. And

that was probably the most exciting thing of all. Tally was starting to truly feel at home in the show ring.

When Tally and Goose left the ring after their third trip—by then they'd worked out the kinks and had no significant, or even insignificant, errors—Ryan held up both his arms dramatically.

"What? You guys keep getting better. That was just awesome," he said. The results from the over fences classes were announced during the under saddle. Goose came in third, second, and first in his trips. Lining up for their results in the hack, Tally felt really fulfilled. The work at home paid off, the nerves faded away, and she and her partner were in the zone together.

"First place goes to number 608, Goose, ridden by Tally Hart. This pair will also end up champion in the children's small/medium pony hunters. Congratulations."

Mac picked up Tally's blue, red, and yellow champion ribbon and joined her outside the ring. They took Goose to the food stand—currently stocked with apple slices and puffy mints—and bought him a bunch of treats for a job well done. They took their time walking back to the Field Ridge setup, letting Goose graze whenever he felt like it.

Once they arrived back at the trailer, Mac and Lupe showed Tally how to load the pony in. Tally gave Goose one last hug for the day.

"You are the best boy," she told him, rubbing behind his ears in his favorite spot. "Thank you for making me feel like a star."

Tally walked down the trailer ramp, grabbed her backpack, and went to find her mom, who had become fast friends with Mac's mother. There was

no telling where those two could be on the show grounds, she thought with a smile.

"Great job again today, Tal," came Ryan's booming voice from the side of the trailer.

"Oh, hey, thank you, Ryan."

"So, there is a possibility—a slim one, but still a chance—that I could have some potential buyers for Goose at Pony Finals next month in Kentucky. I'll talk to your parents about it, but I'd like you to come."

Tally's breath caught in her throat. G could be sold that quickly?

"I want you to come jump him around those big rings. They have ticketed schooling down there, and it will be more valuable mileage for the pony. And people can try him while we're there as well."

"That sounds great. I'd love to see Pony Finals, and anything you need with Goose, I'm happy to do it."

"Thanks, Tal. I know it's hard not to get attached to sales ponies. There will be more, though. Like I said the other day, you've got such natural talent and a feel for the animals. I'm gonna do my best to keep you riding lots, okay?"

Tally smiled and nodded. Crying in front of the trainer who gave her this great opportunity would be pretty poor form. So she swallowed the choked-up feeling and thanked Ryan. Somehow, when the time came, she'd have to reconcile how much she loved G with letting him go.

12

On a Monday morning in August, Tally walked down the boarder aisle on her way to the school side for her working student shift. Like many show barns, Field Ridge was closed for riding on Mondays. It was a built-in, guaranteed day off for the horses each week, a day off for Lupe, and a chance for Ryan to catch up on billing and other non-mounted business.

But since Tally was at the barn to work anyway, she took the opportunity to give her favorite horses on the Field Ridge aisle a pat and a treat. Everyone was happily munching on hay in their stalls, and Tally paused for a few minutes toward the end of the aisle, where Joey and G were stabled right next to each other. Both had mesh stall guards so they could look out over the aisle. Unlike a lot of ponies—the type that Mac described as "spicy"—Joey and Goose could be trusted to get along with each other. And not to bite any passersby, either!

When it was time for her shift to start, Tally gave each of the boys one last pat and turned the corner for the school aisle. She jumped a little bit when she practically ran into Brenna, who was standing at the top of the aisle, right by Sweetie's stall. Her face was lined with worry.

"What's wrong?" Tally asked, joining Brenna in front of her favorite school horse's stall. Inside, the

little mare had a considerable amount of straw in her mane and tail. She'd obviously been rolling, and she looked sweaty.

"I saw her biting at her stomach as I walked by," an instructor named Jamie told Brenna without taking her eyes off the horse.

"Let's get her walking. Tally, please hand walk her around the paths outside but don't let her graze, okay?"

"Got it," Tally said. "You're worried about colic?"

"Yeah, if a horse is impacted then they can sometimes behave like this. Movement helps a lot. I'll get some Milk of Magnesia for her, too."

"The horses at my old barn seemed to like cherry the best. Or, I should say, they disliked it the least," said Jamie.

Tally put Sweetie's halter on and led the mare out

of the stall. Sweetie pinned her ears back halfway as they walked. Of course, this wasn't exactly out of the ordinary for her. Tally led the mare along the gravel walkways outside, sizing up Sweetie's sweaty coat. It was so hot and humid out, she wasn't sure that the sweat was too unusual either.

After a full lap, up toward the rings and then back down the hill, Brenna appeared outside with milky fluid in a fat syringe.

"I promise this is for your own good, Sweetie," she said. She added to Tally, "Hold tight on the lead rope under her chin."

Tally choked up on the lead, scratching the mare's forehead to try to keep her head down. Sweetie downed the liquid messily—Tally caught some drips on her paddock boots—but was pretty compliant about swallowing it.

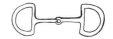

"Atta girl, all done. That should help keep her from getting any more bound up, too," Brenna said. "Another couple of laps would be great if you're not frying out here, Tal."

"No problem," Tally replied. "Anything for Sweetie."

Three more laps and the mare didn't make any moves to stop and poop. Tally reported the lack of progress to Brenna, who suggested a little indoor turnout for Sweetie.

"Let her go in the small indoor and just call me if you see anything alarming, like excessive pawing or digging at the footing, or more biting at her belly."

Tally nodded and brought the mare to the small arena, while Brenna rearranged some of the riding school lessons in the other rings.

After another ten minutes of watching the mare

walk around the ring, not doing much of anything, Tally was happy to see Jacob join her on the rail.

"Hey, Brenna told me you were here. How's Sweetie doing?"

"Fine, I think. Not pooping, but not doing anything more to scare me, so that's good," Tally said with a dry laugh. "Hey, how did you end up doing at the show?"

"Good," Jacob said. "We got ribbons in all our classes, and there were a lot at that height so I was really happy."

"That's great, I'm so happy for you guys. Hey, look!"

Just then, Sweetie stopped her walk down the long side of the ring to casually go to the bathroom, as though several people hadn't been waiting hours for her to do so.

"Yay, Sweetie!" Jacob hollered and Tally laughed, relieved that Sweetie. . .well, relieved herself.

"I swear," Tally said once she'd caught her breath, "horses can scare you half to death."

"Tell me about it," said Jacob. "I'm going to go get mine ready. See you around, Tal."

Once Tally's shift had wrapped up, she put a bridle on Goose and nothing else, walking him up to the large indoor. Ryan had suggested a light bareback ride to see how G would react, and Tally was excited to try something new with the pony.

She found Ryan, Mac, and Joey in the large outdoor ring, with Mac practicing for the model. The regular pony hunter divisions always had an element where the animals were judged on conformation—the way the pony is put together. Tally typically zoned out a little during this part of watching her friend at shows. It wasn't set up in a way that was much fun to watch as a spectator.

"Hey, Tal," Ryan said when she got to the gate. "Hang out a minute before you get on while we wrap up here." Tally gave him a thumbs-up and sat down on the mounting block, holding the buckle of G's reins and watching her friend.

"You can't just stand there like you're walking a dog," Ryan was saying to Mac. "If you work it and Joey does his part, you can affect your score by ten points."

Mac picked up a little handful of footing and threw it up in the air. Joey pricked his ears in response and raised his head a little.

"Good choice there. It's all about posing him to show off his build to the best of our ability, right?"

Mac nodded.

"Okay, now let me see you jog him. No real trick here but to look ahead and run as fast as you can."

Mac ran ahead of Joey, and after a few strides at the walk, he picked up a trot, neck outstretched, and jogged behind her.

"That's fine, Mac. He's usually pretty compliant to jog. Go ahead and put your saddle on—we're going to do a little practice out in the field to replicate what it's going to be like in Kentucky."

Mac smiled at Tally as the girls took turns at the mounting block. "I hope I sweat this much at Pony Finals, too. It's a good look," Mac said with a laugh.

"Tal, you and G are going to be one of the distractions for them while we jump around. The Walnut ring at Pony Finals is like a huge football field set up on a hill. People sit to watch down a little slope, so there's a lot for the ponies to peek and spook at. I'm going to jump Joey and Mac over a few fences in the field, and you just meander around the outside, okay?"

"If Goose has any major objection to being ridden bareback, just hop off. But I think he'll be okay. Let me hold him while you get on. Just do everything slowly and quietly."

Tally was pleasantly surprised to find that getting on a small pony bareback from a three-step mounting block was no big deal at all. She could easily just lift her leg over and settle down super quietly on his back.

It had been quite a while since she'd ridden bareback, but she instantly recalled the amazing feeling of being so close to the horse or pony. She wrapped her legs gently around Goose's sides and he flicked both ears back at her but didn't move otherwise.

"Atta boy. Not a lot fazes you, huh?" Ryan used his knuckles to rub the pony on his forehead. "Okay, Mac, hop on your pony and let's head on down."

Tally squeezed G forward with her legs, unable to suppress a little laugh when he started walking. You could feel everything when riding bareback, each movement of the horse's shoulders, their back muscles, each little tic. It was just too much fun.

Tally walked all the way around the field, gently reminding Goose that he couldn't drop his head to graze as they watched Mac race through the field on Joey.

"That's what ring pace is going to feel like in the Walnut!" Ryan called to Mac. "Get these two verticals one more time, keeping your canter the same."

Tally asked Goose to trot and giggled again

when he picked up the new gait. Keeping her hips and thighs relaxed, she felt herself move from side to side as the pony traveled. Ryan was right—Goose was totally unbothered by Tally on his back without a saddle.

"You are such a special pony, you know that?" Tally said to G as they eased back down to a walk. "You're going to make your new rider really happy."

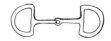

13

Tally's mom and Mac's mom planned the trip down to Kentucky for Pony Finals, and all four were excited to fly out together on a Wednesday morning. It felt like a party up in the sky, the moms and the girls chatting away. They had a lot of ground to cover, after all.

"So you're saying any pony that's champion or reserve at an A show any time during the year is qualified?" Tally asked her friend once they were settled into their airplane seats.

"Yes, that's part of why there are so many ponies there. I think it was like a hundred and fifty mediums last year."

"So even though we wouldn't be ready or anything, Goose technically qualified for Pony Finals since he's been champion at an A show?"

"No, because the children's ponies is a C-rated division, even if it's at an A show. The regular pony divisions are A rated. But if Goose gets sold to a kid who wants to do the small greens next year and they are champion or reserve at an A show, then Goose could qualify for Pony Finals next year in the small greens. That division is actually a lot smaller, too," said Mac. "Ponies can only do their green division for a year, so there are fewer showing than in the regulars."

Tally squeezed her eyes shut for just a moment, as if she was willing the thought of G getting sold out of her brain.

"Sorry," Mac said quickly. "I'm sure that's something you don't want to think about."

"That's okay," Tally said. "It is what it is. Tell me more about a show where there are a hundred and fifty in a division! Are you even thinking about where you'll place?"

"No, I'm really not," Mac said, tightening her seat belt when prompted by the flight attendant. "If we have a solid trip, I'll be really happy. My mom is calling Pony Finals our 'one and done.' It's a lot for just one show, and we may only do it this one year. You get one trip. One! In the biggest, spookiest ring. And that counts for fifty percent of your overall score. Then it's twenty-five percent for the model and twenty-five percent for the under saddle."

"I can't wait to see it," Tally said, mentally pinching herself because she was going to Pony Finals, even if only to watch her friend and ride Goose in ticketed schooling rounds. Ryan, Lupe, and the two ponies arrived on Tuesday night. Joey and Goose would get settled in one of the show barns at Kentucky Horse Park, and then Ryan and Lupe would check in to their hotel. The girls and their moms would arrive Wednesday around lunchtime, with Joey set to show on Friday.

"It's honestly not like any other horse show," Mac said. "I came with my old barn last year, just to watch. Every single rider has to wear their pony's number any time they're on the show grounds. And there is no waiting and no being late. If you miss your section or your order in the class, that's it, you don't show. The place is huge, too, so there's a ton of planning for being where you need to be and when."

"Why is it so strict?" Tally asked.

"Just the number of ponies," said Mac. "You'd never get through them all if the person at the in-gate let it slide when someone was late."

Once the plane reached its cruising altitude, Tally closed her eyes and thought back to horse showing just a year ago. She'd been riding Sweetie in the barn's at-home schooling show series and dreaming about competing in the equitation medal class in addition to her hunter division. It was crazy to think about all that had happened since then, from falling off at her first A show on Danny, to all the success she'd found with Goose. Ryan's pep talk the other day, about having more ponies for her to ride after G, meant a lot. It was starting to feel less like each special ride could be her last and more like anything was possible.

The flight to Kentucky was short and smooth. The moms turned around from time to time to ask their daughters horse show questions. When they landed, Tally and Mac followed their moms to the rental car counter on the ground level of the airport. They piled in a silver sedan and headed off to the show grounds. It was early enough that they could go see the ponies and check things out at the horse park before checking in to their hotel.

Neither one of the girls wore riding clothes for the flight—their first visit to the horse park would be strictly on foot. Tally was so eager to see Goose and to make sure he'd settled in comfortably. Inside the show grounds, once Mac and Tally checked in and got their numbers (Goose had one too for his ticketed rounds), Tally could hardly believe the scene around her. Mac was right: this was unlike any other horse

show she'd seen—in person, in videos, or otherwise.

The Kentucky Horse Park was like its own little city, with tons of barns and pathways and enormous riding rings. There were golf carts everywhere—lines of them backed up in traffic at the pathway intersections. Everyone was in a hurry, and it was so hot.

"Crazy place, right?" said Ryan from the front of the Field Ridge golf cart. Ryan zipped the girls up the hill toward the rings while the moms sat down together to get a bite to eat under the shade of a big tree.

Ryan and the girls went around a bend and drove up to two big rings with what looked like show courses set up.

"It doesn't look that big," Tally whispered to Mac over the crunching of the gravel under their cart.

"That's not the Walnut," Mac said, scanning the

pair of rings along with Tally.

"We'll do a ticketed round here tomorrow, Tal," Ryan said. He was holding his hand over his phone. "Give me just a minute, girls," he said, jumping out of the golf cart and leaving Tally and Mac to watch the ring.

A girl who looked younger than Tally was piloting a buckskin pony to a two-stride, but the pony chipped in and added a stride in the middle.

The trainer yelled something to the rider that Tally and Mac could not make out, and the pony came around again. But they didn't have enough pace. Tally could tell just by watching. And the pony took the opportunity to stop at the first jump. It wasn't a drive-by, either. This was a hoof-planting, hard stop, and the little girl hit the ground.

But then she just stood up, brushed the dirt off

herself, and walked over to the trainer, who had caught her pony. The rider got a leg up from her trainer and gave the pony several swift kicks. They spun right around to the two-stride, which they jumped with no problem.

"That was kind of amazing," Mac said to Tally, without taking her eyes off the pony.

Tally laughed. "Right? I was just thinking that if it were me, that kind of fall would have been a true disaster. I'd still be on the ground, rethinking my life choices!"

"That's a tough kid," added Mac.

"Sorry, guys, I'm back. Let's go up to the Walnut." Ryan put the golf cart into drive before he was even fully sitting down.

They zipped through the massive showgrounds and started up a hill. Tally could see the Walnut ring looming over them. There was no mistaking this one. Once they reached the top of the hill, she could peer down into the massive ring. It looked like a giant, shallow bowl with stands on one side and white letters spelling out 'PONY FINALS' in the grass. A series of flags lined the border between the ring and the road below.

"Well, it is big," Tally said dryly, and Mac laughed. "Has Joey ever been in that ring?"

"No, but we're going to flat in it tomorrow so at least he'll see it," Mac said. "Take a little tour." The golf cart had reached the top of the hill, and they were rolling along slowly behind another cart, piled with riders. A sign that read "No Golf Carts Past This Point" was apparently merely a suggestion, as people drove past it anyway. From up above the Walnut ring, Tally could see rows of vendors,

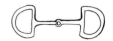

bounce houses, kid-sized jumps like the ones at the tack shop, and even a Slip 'N Slide.

"Let's watch a few of the larges go," Ryan said, gesturing for the girls to follow him to where the Large Pony over fences class was underway in the Walnut.

The ring was a vast expanse of fancy-looking show jumps, greenery, and long stretches of, well, nothing. Tally watched the pony on course cantering down a bending line and balking at something he saw. There was no shortage of sights for a pony to spook at in this ring.

"You must be in here for a full five minutes to get over all the jumps," she whispered to Mac. Ryan began going over the course with Mac, and Tally watched a few more rounds. Two ponies in a row gawked at the second jump in the bending line. And in a few places, there were two identical fences right next to one another, giving the rider the option of which to jump.

"Remember, we'll make a careful plan and walk the course together, too," Ryan was telling Mac. "Every year you'll see at least a couple kids get indecisive about which jump to pick and steer their pony straight into the middle standard. We'll try to avoid that, for starters."

All around them, the crowd seemed to have become hushed. The pony in the ring, a sturdy-looking gray who moved beautifully across the ground, like he was barely even touching it, was having a great round.

When the pony landed off the final fence, a burst of applause erupted through the crowd. When the next pony was over its second jump, the announcer shared the good news for the previous trip: panel

one had scored it an 84, panel two gave it an 81, and panel three gave it an 86.

The group watched several more rounds. The ponies that scored in the 80s were the standouts—most trips had at least one major mistake.

"This is the most equal-opportunity horse show of all the finals," Ryan told them. "The kid on the average pony can ride the pants off the course and beat the top ones. There are just so many opportunities for mistakes at this show."

Mac swallowed audibly and Ryan elbowed her with a little laugh. "That should take the pressure off, kiddo," he said. "Whatever happens, happens. You've got to think of this as any normal class at any normal horse show. You have one shot in this ring. If you have a solid trip, awesome. If not, we'll regroup for the next show and you can still check

Pony Finals off your bucket list."

Mac and Tally watched another twenty-plus trips while Ryan answered texts and calls on his phone and chatted with acquaintances outside the Walnut ring. There were a lot of major mistakes, from chips to stops.

"See that? You get those chips when you lean up because it throws the pony off balance," Mac told her. "I had that issue with my old pony as I got taller. You can get away with it when you're little but then you start to affect the pony more."

She took a deep breath and smiled at Tally.

"I'm not doing Devon nerves again, I told you! This is just another horse show."

"That's right!" Tally said.

"You know what else? We've watched a ton of kids go and, I never really noticed this before,

but everyone is a different size. Isabelle was right. There's skinny and there's athletic and there's bigger riders and smaller ones. But we've seen all different types of riders put in good trips, just sitting here today. So, I'm putting aside that 'fuller' comment."

"Good!" Tally said. "Don't put it aside, though, put it right in the trash."

14

The next morning at seven, Tally's mom drove the girls from the hotel to the horse park. Both wore clothes to school the ponies, their paddock boots and half chaps impeccably clean—there was no misunderstanding Ryan on that point.

Tally would have a ticketed schooling round in one of the pretty, show-like rings they'd seen yesterday. And Mac had a warm-up round in the one right next to it. Ryan scheduled them close together, and the girls left plenty of time to ride the ponies from the barn to the rings.

When the girls arrived at the barn, Joey and Goose had their heads out over their stall doors to greet the riders. Tally had been disappointed to only have a little time with G yesterday. She'd given him a bath and let him graze a little, but today they would have more time together.

"Hey, guys!" Mac said. Both ponies replied with soft nickers. Tally produced a pair of peppermints, picked up from the hotel restaurant.

Tally let herself into G's stall and slipped his shipping halter on, leading him out to graze and stretch his legs a bit before getting tacked up.

By 8:00 a.m., Lupe had both ponies tacked up, saddles and bridles gleaming from the previous afternoon's scrubbing. Ryan insisted that every piece of horse equipment was as tidy as the riders' boots, so Tally and Mac had cleaned their tack before heading to the hotel.

"It's a long walk to the ring. You two can get going as soon as you're ready," Lupe said. Tally let out a little squeal as she flipped her hairnet-covered ponytail up on top of her head and pulled her helmet down over it. Getting to go on a trail ride of sorts just to get to the ring was an added bonus.

Lupe pulled a mounting block out from the tack stall, and the girls swung up into the saddles and set off for the schooling rings.

"I think we're going to ride twice today," said Mac, letting her reins go slack for Joey to check out the showgrounds. "I'll hack in the Walnut after the over fences is done for the day, and I'm sure Ryan will have you take Goose on a tour around the horse park, too."

"I'm star struck by that Walnut ring, just walking

around it. I can't imagine what this guy will think when he sees all the crowds and flags," Tally said, scratching G on the neck. Like Joey, his head was swiveling this way and that, but neither pony acted spooky. Just highly interested.

By the time they got to their ticketed schooling rings, both ponies had a light coating of sweat on their necks. It was just as hot in Kentucky as it was back home, but a whole lot more humid.

"You're first for the warm-up, Mac Attack," Ryan greeted the girls when they walked toward the ring. "Tally, how was Goose on the walk here?"

"Good. Lots to look at but he's happy and quiet."

"Great," Ryan said. "You can let him walk in that ring up there," he said, pointing to a long but somewhat narrow ring with plain white schooling jumps. "There's going to be a lot of traffic, which it can't hurt for him to see. Just stay out of the way of anyone jumping. You can walk around the outside of these rings, too. Just let him check stuff out. I don't mind if he has a bite of grass here or there, but keep it to a minimum. Mac, you go in and start trotting around. Get him bending and moving off your leg right away."

Tally did as Ryan asked, stealing glances at her friend's warm-up when she could. Joey looked relaxed, and Mac looked like she was having fun.

Tally and Goose meandered around the big, plain ring, which seemed to clear out quickly. Next, Tally walked a long lap along the outside of the fence line. Goose peeked around corners a bit and let out a couple of big sighs. It felt like they were still building up their partnership and trust in each other, a part of the process that Tally loved. Over the hill,

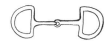

Tally saw Mac walking Joey out of their ring, with Ryan right behind them. The timing was perfect for her to join them.

"Good school?" she asked Mac.

"He's peeking a bit, but good," her friend said.

"Next victim," Ryan joked, nodding at Tally and Goose. "Get to trotting around. Make circles around of each of the jumps. Get him bending and looking at the fences."

Tally started trotting around the ring and smiled as she, too, took a look around. Vendor tents, gazebos, and white fencing surrounded them. It was like riding around in a dream. The fences were all hunter style, with brush and flowers and gates. As interesting as the jumps looked to her, she'd learned over the last few shows that fences like these actually appear very natural and inviting to a horse or pony. It's the stark-looking or the unusual fences that tended to be more spooky. Goose let out a big exhale as they trotted a circle around a birch oxer.

"Once you get back out to the rail, get him trotting nice and forward."

Tally was listening to Ryan and moving the pony back out to the rail when, suddenly, something changed underneath her. Goose felt tense from head to tail, and then, out of nowhere, he stopped dead in his tracks.

Confused about what the pony might be looking at, Tally glanced around, settling on a sweet-looking black pony who was jumping a line toward them.

"Kick him forward, Tal, I think he was just surprised by seeing another pony head on like that."

"Sorry, we've just got one more single and we're out," said the other trainer, a woman in

pink shorts and a big sun hat.

"No problem," Ryan replied with a little wave. "Just working through some greenness here."

Tally worked on her extended trot and then cantered in both directions before Ryan asked her to hop over a low vertical and then halt straight.

Approaching it, Goose still felt a little tense to her.

"Just let that canter flow, Tally, nothing to hold back here. Teeny gate. Just go on with it, keep him moving forward."

Tally let out a big exhale and could feel the pony relax underneath her. They cantered up over the gate and Goose was happy to halt quietly just four strides away.

"Nice. Make a little half circle out to the side here and come back over it the other way."

Tally noticed the other ponies at the gate first, but

when she felt G take notice, she lowered her hand and put her leg on stronger. The pony responded by stepping into a slightly bigger canter. They found a great distance to the little gate going the other way and stopped a few strides after landing.

The rest of the ticketed schooling felt like any lesson at home. Ryan started them off with a bending line, then they jumped a full course a couple of times. Goose felt so tuned in to Tally that she focused purely on keeping herself relaxed and keeping the pony moving forward.

"Really nice job, come on out," Ryan said when they were done schooling. "I'm actually glad he stopped like that when the other pony was coming toward him."

"Sorry, you said you're glad about it?" asked Tally, slightly out of breath. The humidity was oppressive.

"Yes, because a pony has to do these things—stopping, looking, all of that—in order for us to respond to them, right? You responded by staying calm and moving him forward, so he learned something important today. 'Weird thing happens in the ring? That just means I should listen to my rider.' See what I mean?"

Tally nodded, patting Goose's neck and feeling a rush of pride for helping teach the pony.

"I've got someone trying him tomorrow in the morning. I'll have you flat him around first so they can watch him go, and then the kid will get on and have a little lesson with her trainer. We can hang back and watch."

Tally handed Goose off to Lupe after one last cuddle. Mac would be flatting Joey in the Walnut ring later in the day and Tally would take Goose on that long walk around the grounds then. But they had plenty of time in between.

Mac and Tally met up to eat, and Mac introduced Tally to some girls from her old barn. They were engaged in a spirited conversation about their Snapple bottles. One girl read the little factoid inside the cap to another.

"Why do you put your tongue in the bottle before you drink it?" Mac asked, playfully teasing one of the girls.

"Yeah, that's pretty weird," said the other, and all three laughed. Tally always felt a little awkward in situations like this, where she was the only one who didn't know the others, but it was pretty easy to fall into their conversations. Yet again, a shared interest in riding was like a great equalizer, and everyone was effortlessly friendly.

"Ellie showed her pony Bits in the small greens yesterday," Mac told Tally, referring to the blonde girl from her old barn.

"How did it go?" Tally asked her.

"Um, bad. Really bad," Ellie said, but she was smiling. "We knew it was a little early for him to come here, but we wanted to give it a shot. It is a long ride back out of the ring when you have two refusals at the first two jumps," she added with a shrug.

"Everyone under the tent by the in-gate was so supportive though, clapping for you guys," added the other girl, Caroline.

"Yeah, and I think Bits took that applause too literally. He was all, 'I nailed it! When do we jog?'"

All four girls laughed at that.

"They call it the Path of Tears for a reason," said

Caroline, drinking the last of her iced tea.

"What's the Path of Tears?" Tally asked.

"The long walk to and from the Walnut ring," Mac said. "You'll see it when I flat Joey."

"I'm definitely going to sell this show shirt now," Ellie said. "I bought it specifically for today. Obviously it's bad luck, so it's outta here."

"Yeah, but do you want to pass along that bad luck to someone else?" Mac asked. "That's got to be, like, bad karma or something for you."

"Doesn't work like that," Caroline chimed in. "It's specific to the rider. That shirt is safe for someone else, just not for you."

Tally smiled, thinking back on the supposedly lucky socks she'd worn when she showed Danny, which she subsequently swore she'd never wear again.

The girls went back to their respective barns once everyone had finished eating. The day was positively flying by. And while Tally always enjoyed walking show grounds wherever they were showing, there was something extra special about Pony Finals and the Kentucky Horse Park. The atmosphere was so spirited and fun-loving—it was like being transported to a world that revolved around riding. When it was time for Mac to flat in the Walnut, a rare breeze rustled the trees throughout the horse park. Everyone, ponies and people alike, welcomed the movement of summer air all around them.

Mac kept Goose on a long rein as they walked, and he stretched his neck out appreciatively. She got to peek in at Mac in the Walnut ring as they flatted. It really was the biggest ring she'd ever seen, and it was super unique with all the flags and places for spectators to watch. She could see the long trail that led up to the in-gate, too.

It was an awfully long distance to travel if you'd had a bad round.

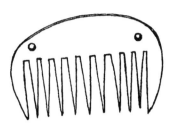

15

The next morning, Tally expected Mac to be serious, if not downright nervous, in the hotel room, but Mac simply looked excited.

"I can't believe I'm in the first section," Mac said. "It's actually great, though. Waiting around is so hard." She stifled a yawn. It was four thirty in the morning and Mac would be modeling Joey in that first group beginning at seven o'clock sharp, and then would move into their under saddle class.

While Mac put on her show shirt, breeches, and

garter straps, Tally dressed in show breeches and a plain blue polo shirt, tucked in and topped with a stretchy belt. Tally wanted to look professional for the people trying Goose.

The girls and their moms piled into the rental car quietly, as though trying not to disturb anyone still sleeping in the hotel. They arrived at the horse park fifteen minutes later and went straight to the barn where the Field Ridge ponies were stabled. Mac and Ryan talked a bit, and Tally slipped into Goose's stall. He was lying down, his forelock adorned with shavings.

"Could you be any cuter?" Tally asked with a laugh, squatting down next to the pony. "Don't get up! I brought you a hotel apple." She made Goose eat it in a few bites, rather than letting him wolf the whole thing down.

At 6:00 a.m., Ryan and Lupe had the golf cart packed with Mac's show jacket, saddle, and show pad. Lupe led Joey on the long walk to the ring, while the girls rode with Ryan. The show grounds were still waking up, the quiet surroundings punctuated now and again by a whinny or a trainer calling out instructions.

Tally found a spot along the rail with Lupe to watch the first group of ponies model as the announcer called for the ponies to stand "head to tail on the line." It was all a lot more elaborate than she'd seen at their shows back home.

The kids were dressed in their riding clothes, including their helmets, even though no one would be mounted in this particular class. Most of the ponies had on those thick, fake tails that were typical for big shows. The riders were working hard to perfect the ponies' positioning and expressions.

"They all seem to stand just right on their own," Tally said to Lupe.

"Yeah, the ones who show in the big-time know how to stand themselves up," Lupe told her. "But the rider still needs to get that good expression out of them and jog them in front of the judges. Joey can be a stinker about the model."

"He can?"

"Yes. Hopefully not today, but we will see."

Joey was lined up in the middle of the pack and looked content, even a little sleepy. Though Mac tried to get the pony's attention here and there, Tally could tell she was waiting until the judges came over to pull out her bag of tricks.

When the judges were just a pony or two away, Joey developed an itch on his belly, behind his front

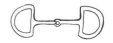

leg. And it had to be scratched right at that moment.

"Oh, no," she heard Lupe whisper, and he ran his hands down his face.

"Right now? He's choosing to scratch his belly right now?" Tally asked. But Mac shook her head and smiled.

Just as the judges headed toward Joey, he gave the spot on his belly one last swipe with his teeth. Mac quickly dug her fingers into that spot herself, itching it for him. Joey responded by sticking his head straight up in the air and flipping his top lip up for a moment. He followed that with a quick, full-body shake, before settling in to model.

"Oh, Joey!" Lupe whispered, and Tally laughed. It did, however, look like the pony would get his act together just in time.

Mac stood with one leg bent in front of her and

the other straight behind, moving something around in her fingers to get Joey's attention. He pricked his ears forward, doing his part. The photographer snapped away the whole time, and Joey held his calm, alert expression. Lupe seemed relieved. When it was Mac's turn to jog the shiny chestnut (his coat was really gleaming in the early morning sunlight), he trotted behind her happily as usual.

Lupe said something into his walkie talkie and then turned to Tally. "See ya back for the hack, yeah?" Tally nodded. She had a long walk around to the other side of the Walnut ring, and Lupe had to saddle the pony and make sure Mac looked her best for their next class.

Tally walked behind the big VIP tents, all the way around to the Path of Tears, but the ponies weren't lined up to hack yet. She stood in line to buy a

smoothie, overhearing a trainer talk to a mom about the medium pony over fences class the next day.

"They jump in reverse order," the trainer was saying. "She got a solid score in the model so if she hacks well too, we'll jump later in the day. If she scores low in the hack, she'll jump earlier."

Once Tally had her strawberry-banana smoothie in hand, she made her way back toward the fence line on the other side of the Walnut ring. It had been divided in two for the model on one side, the under saddle on the other. She made it back just in time.

"Section one of our medium ponies, please come on in to the rail."

Mac and Joey walked into the ring together, Joey's hooves shining from well-timed applications of hoof polish.

"Spread out and trot, please, riders," said the

announcer. Mac invisibly asked Joey to trot and he responded in his usual, floaty style, as though he was barely touching the ground. Most of the other ponies had little or no white on their legs, so Joey's high, white socks were particularly eye-catching. Obviously, markings didn't win ribbons for ponies, but it was hard to ignore it when a pony looked as flashy as Joey.

There were about a dozen mediums in this section. Tally noticed that a couple ponies seemed annoyed when their fake tails got caught in between their hind legs. Others, including Joey, held their tails up high so that they floated and bounced behind them.

It might have been Pony Finals, but this was still your typical under saddle class. Walk, trot, walk, canter. Reverse direction. At the end of the class, though, the ponies were asked to halt out of their

canter, something you didn't always see in the show ring. These ponies knew the drill, though. Everyone halted promptly and quietly.

Tally had no idea how a judge would begin to order so many gorgeous ponies.

When the first section of mediums lined up for the judges to take a final look, the second section began walking in. This show was choreographed to the last detail, and it was impressive to watch. Tally met Mac and Joey at the bottom of the hill below the Walnut ring. Mac looked really happy.

"Hey, you guys looked great!" Tally said.

"Thanks," Mac answered, smiling. "Ryan was happy with how both classes went for us. So now. . .we wait! I honestly don't care so much about our scores. I just hope we have a good course tomorrow. I'll be so happy if we get around and we're solid."

Tally walked back to their barn alongside Joey and Mac, who stayed mounted. She took Goose out to graze until Ryan asked her, via Lupe, to get him ready for the trial. Tally bit her lip. She couldn't even think about tearing up right now. She had a job to do for Ryan. Plus, he said it was only an outside chance that G would get snapped up at Pony Finals. Maybe this would just be practice for other trials on the pony.

Back at the schooling rings, Tally trotted and cantered Goose in both directions and popped over both outside lines. Ryan didn't have much to say to her; he seemed busy chatting with the potential buyer and her trainer. For his part, Goose acted like he'd been cantering around this ring his whole life.

"Come on over, Tal," Ryan called to her from the middle of the ring. "Go ahead and hop off.

Tally, this is Olivia. Olivia, Tally."

"Hi," Tally said, "nice to meet you."

"You too," the little girl replied. Her trainer swapped out Tally's saddle for Olivia's—Tally went to grab hers but Lupe was already in the ring to take it from them. In just a matter of seconds, this new rider was up on Goose's back, trotting around.

Olivia had a short lesson with her trainer, and G was pretty close to perfect for them. Olivia pet the pony's neck over and over again when they were finished. Tally could tell she liked him. Olivia walked the pony over to Tally when she was done. Ryan and the trainer chatted some more while Tally loosened G's girth and gave him a big, appreciative pat.

"You can take him to Lupe. Thanks for your help, Tal," Ryan said, and the other trainer thanked her as well.

Tally handed the pony to Lupe and gazed at the ring once more. Were these going to be Goose's new owners?

At dinner that night, Tally and Mac discussed the news from the day with their moms. They knew the biggest piece of news already: Joey came in fourteenth place overall in the under saddle. Out of a hundred and fifty ponies! Everyone knew he was a good mover, but it was still exciting to hear that he did that well out of such a huge field. Mac carried the lime green ribbon with her the rest of the day. Tally didn't blame her. This was a show where ribbons were quite hard to come by!

"So, what's the deal with tomorrow?" Mac's mom asked. "When will you go? And where is Joey in the standings?"

"With Joey's combined hack and model scores,

he's jumping 124th tomorrow. Which means he's 26th place overall out of the one hundred and fifty. Ryan says a great trip could move us up a lot. There's just so much room for error in that ring."

"Easy with the ribbon pressure there, Mac Attack," Tally said with a little laugh.

"I know. I'm not actually nervous or putting pressure on us," said Mac. "I never expected to get any ribbon at Pony Finals, so the fact that we got one in the hack is amazing.

"What about you, Tally? What's on the schedule for Goose tomorrow?" Mac's mom asked.

Tally told the group about Ryan's report: The buyers were quite interested in Goose. Another prospective buyer would be trying G the next morning, and a few hours later, Olivia would be riding him again.

"It's great timing," Tally added, "because Mac

won't show over fences until the afternoon. And, obviously, I can't miss her!"

"You're being so mature about all this sales talk," Tally's mom said.

Mac's mom nodded. "It's got to be hard knowing he could get sold while we're here."

"It is," said Tally, taking a knife to cut her newly-arrived chicken sandwich in half. "But it's not like it's a surprise. I've known for a while that he could possibly get sold here."

Everyone had dessert and got to bed by nine o'clock. A good night's sleep would be essential for the last full day at Pony Finals.

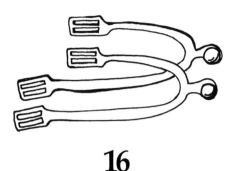

16

Tally and Mac were hand-grazing their ponies by eight the next morning.

"How are you feeling about today?" Tally asked Mac. Both girls leaned up against their ponies as they grazed, enjoying the relative cool before the August sun would come out in full force.

"Really good. It's been so much fun to turn things around from Devon and not make it about the pressure this time," Mac said, adjusting her blonde ponytail into a messy bun. "I'm sweating like crazy already, are you?"

"No, but any minute now," Tally said with a laugh.

Lupe walked over with updates for the girls. He told Mac that Ryan wanted her to take Joey for a long walk before the pony's pre-show bath.

"You can tack up Goose and walk him over to the ring for the trial, Tal," he added. Tally took her time tacking the pony and then settled into the saddle for their long, loose walk to the ring.

Today's prospective buyers looked a lot like the ones from the day before. This rider was smaller than Olivia, though, and struck Tally as timid right from the start. Ryan asked Tally to trot and canter Goose a couple of laps in both directions to warm him up. They were schooling in the annex ring today—the long, narrow one. There was plenty of time down those long sides for Goose to show off his pretty

movement. They also popped over a couple of plain white verticals before the new little rider got on.

Ryan asked the trainer if they wanted to do a ticketed round in one of the rings with the full courses just down the hill, but the trainer was content with a short trial in the plain ring. Tally wondered whether that meant they weren't very interested. The little rider looked good on G. He had a way of making all his riders look good, she noticed. The rider was definitely more timid than the pony was used to at the jumps, and she even caught G in the mouth a bit on the landing side of the verticals. He swished his tail when she did that, but didn't even pin his ears. Such a gentleman, Tally thought wistfully.

Ryan and the other trainer talked for quite a while as the rider walked G around the ring on a loose rein.

"Thanks, guys," Ryan said to them. "Call or text

anytime." The rider dismounted and handed the reins to Tally with a shy smile, which Tally returned.

"Change of plans, Tal," Ryan said in a low voice as the girl and her trainer walked away. "The buyers from yesterday are coming in just a few minutes to try Goose again. Do you mind hanging out with him here until they arrive?"

"I don't mind," Tally said, trying not to let her mind twist itself into knots over what this change in schedule might mean.

"Great. Lupe, come put his halter on, please, and see if he wants some water. Tal, just let the pony graze until they get here and we'll re-tack him."

On a grassy patch between the rings, Goose swallowed some water from a bucket and dug into the thick grass. Tally scratched his withers. That was another one of his favorite spots, she'd recently

discovered while bathing him.

The next trial unfolded a lot like Olivia's first. This time, Tally wasn't needed for riding. Olivia took G into the ring with the full course for another ticketed schooling trip. She wore small, rounded spurs, and G jumped up a little higher and harder than usual. He swapped in front of one of the fences on the course the trainer had made up, but otherwise the pony looked totally solid.

"Heading back to the barn, Tally. You want to come?" Lupe asked her.

Ryan gave her a nod. "Go ahead, Tal, hang out with Mac, look at the course with her again. I'll meet you guys back at the barn when we're done here."

Because Tally's saddle was positioned next to Lupe in the driver's seat, Tally sat in one of the rear seats on the golf cart, facing backward. She watched

Ryan, G, Olivia, and Olivia's trainer get smaller and smaller as they drove away. Tally was still managing to keep herself somewhat detached from the process. Goose wasn't ever going to be hers, and he would get sold eventually. The particulars didn't really matter.

Down at the barn, Tally found Mac wiping down her saddle and bridle.

"Hey, want to go meet those girls again for an early lunch?"

"Sure," Tally said. "I also want to get a Pony Finals souvenir from the vendor tents, but I don't want to walk three miles to get up there. Think Ryan will let us drive the golf cart?"

"Ha!" Mac said loudly as she replaced the saddle on its rack and twisted her bridle into a figure-eight. "He rarely gives up that kind of control. Especially

when you're still, like, three years away from getting your license."

"Fair point," Tally said, smiling. "Let me just change into sneakers instead of these boots."

After lunch, Mac got changed into her show clothes to walk the course with Ryan. It was extremely rare to walk a hunter course the way jumper and equitation riders did. But in the Walnut ring, Tally was learning, all bets were off. It was just a completely different experience for ponies and riders. After the course walk, Ryan produced a pair of VIP wristbands for the girls to wear in the big tent perched above the Walnut ring.

"These are from a trainer who I'm friends with, Laura. You've met her, Mac. Have a snack, and drink lots of water to stay hydrated. You can watch a bunch of ponies go while you're sitting in the shade."

Underneath the VIP tent, the girls spooned fruit salad into paper bowls, grabbed icy water bottles from a cooler, and sat down to watch some early rounds in the class. Like the other day, there were several small mistakes—big ones, too, from adding strides, to trotting on course, to flat-out refusals. There were just so many challenges in and around this ring, and it got the better of a lot of ponies.

"I just want to watch a few more go," Mac said after a while. "It's helpful to see how the lines ride. They walk pretty straightforward but it helps to watch ponies actually do it."

After another ten trips and a couple of yogurts, it was time for the girls to make their way back down to the barn.

Over the next hour, Mac got dressed, checking to make sure each detail was just right. The braider

finished up Joey's mane before turning him over to Lupe, who applied the first coat of hoof oil and ran a clean rag over the pony's coat. The moms had taken over the VIP spots to watch Mac's round, and Tally and Mac plopped down in the back of the golf cart with Ryan up front. Lupe walked the pony to the warm-up area.

After a quick flat and jumping a couple of verticals, then a pair of oxers, Ryan deemed Joey and Mac ready to go. The group rode and drove over to the bottom of the long path leading up to the Walnut ring, where a copy of the course diagram was posted.

"Let's go over the course one more time," Ryan said to Mac. The blazing sun of the early afternoon had tucked itself away behind a layer of clouds, leaving Mac and Joey with a hazy—but thankfully not shadowy—light for their course.

"So, you'll trot in, let him look at those jumps on the end of the ring, then pick up your canter on the long side, just after the outside line. Get your ring pace right away. I don't want him behind your leg at all going to the first jump. You've got that option at jump one, so, stick to your plan and jump the outside option. Land and look left so he knows where he's going. Keep that forward canter to the outside line, and then there's no set number of strides from jump three to four on the bending line. We walked it in six but it will depend on your track. Same thing as jump one —you're taking the outside option. Think less about the number of strides there and more about maintaining your forward canter. Are ya with me?"

Mac nodded and Tally took a deep breath for her. The ring was massive, and the jumps were all

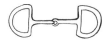

so filled and beautiful. How could she not be at least a little nervous?

"Then, be sure to stay out in your corner before the diagonal. That's what's getting kids here. They're falling in and chipping at jump five. But you'll stay out, keep your pace, and jump the diagonal line in eight strides, then the two-stride. He's so good at those, if you've got the pace, you'll jump out no problem. Then it's six strides up the other outside line and ending on the single oxer coming home. If you've got your ring pace, that'll come right up, and he should land right for you. Just don't be too relaxed after you land, though, so you remember that lead change if you need it."

Mac nodded again, drawing her finger around the course in front of her.

"Let's head up the path here. It'll take a good

half-hour or so," Ryan joked. "Tally, come with us too. The moms can stay in the tent but we'll be Mac's cheering squad at the gate, okay?"

Tally followed Ryan and Lupe, happy to be part of the ringside support squad. Joey lazily swished his tail ahead of them.

By the time they reached the top of the hill, Mac finally looked nervous.

"It's about time," Tally joked to her friend.

"What?"

"That you look even a tiny bit nervous."

Mac smiled tightly. "It's just. . .a lot."

"This is a very intimidating ring," Ryan told her. "But there's no pressure. You have this whole, huge Walnut ring to yourself with your pony. Enjoy it. Keep that canter up. And we'll see you when you're done to celebrate your first Pony Finals."

The ring starter looked at Mac as the pony in the ring cleared its last fence. "Don't be afraid to smile out there, all right? Head on in, girl."

As the previous rider finished her circle, Mac began hers. Joey definitely had his game face on for the occasion. He took in the jumps, to be sure, but this was a pony who knew his job. Tally thought he seemed excited, but focused.

Joey picked up his ground-skimming, straight-legged canter. Tally felt like she could barely watch — she was so nervous for her friend. But once they were on the approach to fence one, the outside option of the double birch vertical, everything seemed to fall into place. Tally let out a big exhale.

"Big relief once you're over the first jump," said Ryan to no one in particular. Joey and Mac landed off their chosen vertical and Joey kept his left lead.

Tally heard Ryan exhale loudly himself.

The pair turned up for the outside line, and the announcer came on to call out the previous rider's scores and introduce Mac.

"Now showing: Smoke Hill Jet Set Set, number 775, the entry owned and ridden by Mackenzie Bennett. Number 775."

By now, Mac and Joey were heading for jump four off Mac's eye. So far, so good. They got to it in the six strides without a problem and then Mac sat down more deeply into her saddle.

"Stay out, stay out," Ryan said in a stage whisper, and his rider did just that. Then Mac turned for the diagonal line to the two-stride, and each jump unfolded perfectly. They were making it look easy. Next up was the outside line going away from the gate. Mac kept up the pony's canter, and they got

those six strides done easily. Now it was down to just the final oxer. Tally glanced at Ryan, who was bending his knees lightly in time with Joey's canter, as if he were riding the course himself. Lupe, who stood next to him, was biting his lower lip.

With just a few strides to go, Tally stood on her tiptoes, ready to applaud her friend for a stellar round. Then Joey took a funny stride close to the final oxer, almost like he'd randomly slipped a little, and jumped up over the fence, making a cracking sound on his way to the ground. Everyone around Tally gasped. Joey had uncharacteristically come down on the back rail of the oxer early with a hind foot.

And like the worst possible punctuation at the end of a gorgeous course at Pony Finals, that back rail came down, hitting the ground with a sickening thud.

17

"Ohhhhhh!" the crowd collectively groaned after that final rail hit the ground. Tally's hand flew to her mouth; Lupe dropped his chin down to his chest, and Ryan kicked the ground with the toe of his boot. This was a massive bummer. But when Mac finished her circle and walked Joey toward the gate, she didn't look unhappy.

"Worst rail in history," she said with a shrug, still rubbing her pony's neck.

"I couldn't have said it better," Ryan replied as

they started walking down the path. "That was one crappy fluke, kiddo. I chalk it up to nothing more than bad luck. He had a weird stumble and then just came down too early on the back side. But can we talk about how awesome your course was up until the very end?"

Mac beamed as Ryan went over his favorite parts of the course. Tally still felt a little disappointed for her friend, but it encouraged her to see what mattered most to Mac, and to Ryan.

Back at the barn, Mac shook out her sweaty hair before scraping it back into a ponytail underneath her new Pony Finals baseball cap she'd purchased earlier in the day. Tally had bought the same one. Mac had a little buffet of carrots, horse cookies, and peppermints for Joey, which he happily gobbled up.

Tally let herself in to Goose's stall, and the pony

pricked his ears at her. She was reminded of when they'd first met. It was like opening a new Breyer horse on Christmas morning. This sweet little green pony had taught her so much in such a short time.

"Thank you, buddy," she whispered to him as he lipped a crumbled horse cookie from her palm. "Thank you for making me a catch rider. I love you so much. I hope we have more time together, but no matter what, you'll be so special to me forever and ever."

Tally spent a while longer in the pony's stall, going over his coat with his favorite soft brush and rubbing his face and withers just the way he liked. When she let herself out of his stall, Ryan had just arrived at the end of the aisle.

"Hey, Tal," he said, his voice gentler than usual. "Those first buyers, the little girl Olivia and her

trainer, they loved Goose. Assuming he passes the vet, they want to move forward with him. Thank you so much for all you've done with him, kiddo."

He reached out his arms for a hug and Tally let him wrap her up. Olivia seemed like a nice girl and a strong rider. Goose would have a great home with her.

But Tally still cried. She cried into Ryan's polo shirt, both of them laughing as he assessed the wet spot on his shoulder. She cried petting Goose as he stuck his head over the stall guard to see what was going on. And then she cried into his neck as she gave him another long hug. It was now, officially, time to move on.

"I love you, my sweet Goose," she told him, giving him a kiss on the nose. "I will never forget you."

Catch up on the *Show Strides* Series

#1 School Horses and Show Ponies

#2 Confidence Comeback

About the Authors

Piper Klemm, Ph.D. is the publisher of *The Plaid Horse* magazine and a partner in The Plaid Horse Network. Additionally, she co-hosts the weekly podcast of The Plaid Horse, the #Plaidcast, and is an adjunct professor at St. Lawrence University. She has been riding since she was eight years old and currently owns a dozen hunter ponies who compete on the horse show circuit. She frequently competes in the adult hunter divisions across North America, so you might see her at a horse show near you!

Rennie Dyball has loved horses ever since she was a little girl. She started taking lessons at age twelve, went on to compete with the Penn State equestrian team, and continues to show in the hunter, jumper, and equitation rings. She spent fifteen years as a writer and editor at *People* magazine and People.com, and has ghostwritten several books. With *Show Strides*, Rennie is thrilled to combine two of her greatest passions—writing and riding.

About the Illustrator

Madeleine Murray grew up in rural Vermont, among horses and working farms. She is a painter and illustrator based in northern New York, as well as an artist-in-residence at *The Plaid Horse* magazine. You can see her paintings at mmurrayart.com.

Who's Who at Quince Oaks

Ava Foster: Friends with Tally and Kaitlyn, used to own Danny but quits riding

Beau: Field Ridge pony who belongs to a rider named Marion

Brenna: Barn manager at Quince Oaks

Carlo: Jacob's horse, a jumper

Cindy Bennett: Mac's mom

Field Ridge: Ryan's business within Quince Oaks

Goose: A green small pony that Tally is catch-riding

Isabelle: Sixteen-year-old who rides with Ryan

Jacob Viston: A jumper rider who trailers in to train with Ryan

James Hart: Tally's dad

Jordan: Takes lessons at Quince Oaks, sometimes with Tally

Kaitlyn Rowe: Tally's best friend at school who also rides

Kelsey: Working student for the riding school

Lupe: Field Ridge's head groom

Mackenzie (Mac) Bennett: Newcomer to the barn who owns Joey

Maggie: Takes lessons at Quince Oaks, sometimes with Tally

Marsha: the barn secretary at Quince Oaks

Meg: Tally's instructor at Quince Oaks before Ryan

Olivia: A rider who tries Goose at Pony Finals

Quince Oaks: The barn

Ryan McNeil: Mackenzie's trainer and Tally's new instructor after Meg leaves the barn

Scout: One of the Quince Oaks school horses

Smoke Hill Jet Set (Joey at the barn): Mac's medium pony hunter

Stacy Hart: Tally's mom

Stonelea Dance Party (Danny at the barn): Formerly Ava Foster's pony, goes up for sale through Ryan

Sweet Talker (Sweetie at the barn): Tally's favorite school horse

Natalia (Tally) Hart: Rides Ryan's sales ponies and in the lesson program at Quince Oaks

Glossary of Horse Terminology

A circuit: Nationally-rated horse shows.

backed: When a horse or pony that's newly in training has a rider on its back for the first time.

base: Where a horse or pony leaves the ground in front of a jump; also: refers the rider's feet in the stirrups, with heels down acting as anchors, or a base of support, for the rider's legs.

bay: A horse color that consists of a brown coat and black points (i.e., black mane, tail, ear edges and legs).

buzzer: The sound in the jumper ring that indicates a horse and rider have 45 seconds to cross the timers in front of the first jump.

canter: A three-beat gait that horses and ponies travel in-it's a more controlled version of the gallop, the fastest of the gaits (which are walk, trot, canter, gallop).

catch-riding: When a rider gets to ride and/or show a horse or pony for someone else.

cavaletti: Very small jumps for schooling, or jumping practice.

chestnut: A reddish brown horse/pony coat color, with a lighter mane and tail.

chip: When a horse or pony takes off too close to a jump by adding in an extra stride near the base.

colic: a catch-all term for gastrointenstinal distress in a horse or pony; can be fatal in severe cases.

colt: A young male horse.

conformation class: A horse show class in which the animals are modeled and judged on their build.

crest release: When the rider places his or her hands up the horse or pony's neck, thus adding slack to the reins and giving the animal freedom of movement in its head and neck.

crop/bat: A small (and humane!) whip that is used behind the rider's leg when the rider's leg aid is not sufficient.

cross-rail: A jump consisting of two rails in the shape of an X.

curry comb: A grooming tool used in circles on a horse or pony's coat to lift out dirt.

Devon: An annual, prestigious invitation-only horse show in Pennsylvania.

diagonal line: Two jumps with a set distance between them set on the diagonal of a riding ring.

distance: The take-off spot for a jump. Riders often talk about "finding distances," which means finding the ideal spot to take off over a jump.

flower boxes: Like "walls," these are jump adornments that are placed below the lowest rail of a jump.

gate: Part of a jump that is placed in the jump cups instead of a rail. Typically heavier than a standard jump rail so horses and ponies can be more careful in jumping

them so as not to hit a hoof.

gelding: A castrated male horse.

girth: A piece of equipment that holds the saddle securely on a horse or pony. The girth attaches to the billets under the flaps of the saddle and goes underneath the horse, behind the front legs, and is secured on the billets on the other side.

green: A horse or pony who has less training and/or experience (the opposite of a "made" horse or pony, which has lots of training and experience).

gymnastic: A line of jumps with one, two, or zero strides between them (no strides in between jumps is called a bounce—and the horse or pony lands off the first jump and immediately takes off for the next without taking a stride).

hack: Can either mean riding a horse on the flat (no jumps) in an indoor ring or outside; or, an under-saddle class at a horse show, in which the animal is judged on its performance on the flat.

hands: A unit of measurement for horse or pony heights. One hand equals 4 inches so a 15-hand horse is 60 inches tall from the ground to its withers. A pony that's 12.2 hands is 12 hands, 2 inches, or 50 inches tall at the withers.

handy: A handy class in a hunter division is meant to test a horse or pony's handiness, or its ability to navigate a course. Special elements included in handy hunter courses may include trot jumps, roll backs and hand gallops.

in-and-out: two jumps with one stride in between, typically part of a jumper or equitation course.

in-gate: Sometimes just referred to as "the gate," it's where horses enter and exit the show ring. Usually it's one gate for both directions; sometimes two gates will be in

use, one to go in and the other to come out.

jog: how ponies and horses in A-rated divisions finish each over fences class; the judge calls them to jog across the ring to check for soundness and orders the class.

jump-off: an element in many jumper classes in which horses and riders jump a shortened course and the fastest time with the fewest jumping and time faults wins.

large pony: A pony that measures over 13.2 hands but no taller than 14.2 hands.

lead changes: Changing of the canter lead from right to left or vice versa. The inside front and hind legs stretch farther when the horse or pony is on the correct lead. A lead change can be executed in two ways: A simple lead change is when the horse transitions from the canter to the trot and then picks up the opposite canter lead. In a flying lead change, the horse changes its lead in midair without trotting.

line: Two jumps with a set number of strides between them.

longe line: A long lead that attaches to a horse's halter or bridle. The horse or pony travels around the handler in a large circle to work on the flat with commands from the handler holding the line.

Maclay: One of the big equitation or "big eq" classes for junior riders. Riders compete in regional Maclay classes to qualify for the annual Maclay Final. The final is currently held at the National Horse Show at the Kentucky Horse Park in the fall.

mare: A mature female horse.

martingale: A piece of tack intended to keep a horse or pony from raising its head too high. The martingale attaches to the girth, between the animal's front legs, and then (in a standing martingale) a single strap attaches to the noseband or (in a running martingale) a pair of straps attach to the reins.

medium pony: A pony taller than 12.2 hands but no taller than 13.2 hands.

outside line: A line of jumps with a set number of strides between them on the long sides of the riding ring. An outside line set parallel to the judges' box/stand is called a judges' line.

oxer: A type of jump that features two sets of standards and two top rails, which can be set even (called a square oxer) or uneven, with the back rail higher than the front. A typical hunter over fences class features single oxers as well as oxers set as the "out" jump in lines.

palomino: A horse or pony with a golden color coat and a white mane and tail.

pinned: The way a horse show class is ordered and ribbons are awarded, typically from first through sixth or first through eight place (though some classes go to tenth or even twentieth place).

polos: Also called polo wraps, they provide protection and support to a horse or pony's legs while being ridden.

pommel: The front part of an English saddle; the rider sits behind this.

Pony Finals: An annual show, currently held at the Kentucky Horse Park, in which ponies who were champion or reserve at an A-rated show are eligible to compete.

posting trot: When a rider posts (stands up and sits down in the saddle) as the horse or pony is trotting, making the gait more comfortable and less bouncy for both the rider and the animal.

quarter sheet: A blanket intended for cold weather riding that attaches under the saddle flaps and loops under the horse or pony's tail.

regular pony hunter division (sometimes called "the division"): A national, or A-rated horse show division in which small ponies jump 2'3, medium ponies jump 2'6, and

large ponies jump 2'9-3'.

rein: The reins are part of the bridle and attach to the horse or pony's bit. Used for steering and slowing down.

sales pony/sales horse: A pony or horse that is offered for sale; trainers often market a sales horse or pony through ads and by showing the animal.

school horses/school ponies: Horses or ponies who are used in a program teaching riding lessons.

schooling ring: A ring at a horse show designated for warming up or schooling.

schooling shows: Unrated shows intended for practice as well as for green horses and ponies to gain experience.

shad belly: A formal show coat with tails typically worn for hunter classics and derbies.

small pony: A pony that measures 12.2 hands and under.

spooky: A horse or pony that's easily spooked or startled.

spurs: An artificial aid, worn on a rider's boots to add impulsion.

stakes class: Part of a hunter division; it's a class that offers prize money.

stirrup irons: The metal loops in which riders place their feet.

stirrup leathers: Threaded through the stirrup bars of the saddle and through the stirrups themselves, the leathers hold the stirrups in place.

swap: When a horse or pony unnecessarily changes its lead on course.

tack: The equipment a horse wears to be ridden (e.g. saddle, bridle, martingale, etc.).

tall boots: The knee-high, black leather boots that hunter/jumper/equitation riders wear with breeches when they reach a certain height or age. Prior to that, riders wear paddock boots (which only reach past the ankles) and jodphurs.

ticketed schooling: Opportunities offered by some horse shows to ride in show rings unjudged, as practice

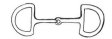

for horses and riders.

trail rides: A ride that takes places out on trails instead of in a riding ring.

transition: When a horse or pony moves from one gait to another, for example, moving from the canter to the trot is a downward transition; moving from the walk to the trot is an upward transition.

trot: A two-beat gait in which the horse or pony's legs move in diagonal pairs.

tricolors: The ribbons awarded for champion (most points in a division) and reserve champion (second highest number of points in that division).

trip: Another term for a jumping round, or course, mostly used at shows, as in, "the pony's first trip."

vertical: A jump that includes one set of standards and a rail or rails set horizontally.

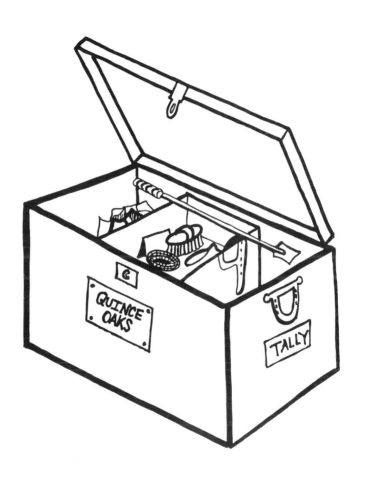

The Plaid Horse encourages every young equestrian to:

- **Read** *The Plaid Horse* magazine and online at theplaidhorse.com/read

    Subscribe at theplaidhorse.com/subscribe

- **Watch** The Plaid Horse Network at network.theplaidhorse.com

    On Roku, AppleTV, The Plaid Horse Network App

    for iOS & Android

- **Listen** to the #Plaidcast, The Podcast of The Plaid Horse at theplaidhorse.com/listen

    On iTunes, Google Play, Stitcher, & Spotify